D1231957

The Wilderness and the City

American Classical Philosophy as a Moral Quest

Michael A. Weinstein

The University of Massachusetts Press   Amherst, 1982

191
W424

Library of Congress Cataloging in Publication Data
Weinstein, Michael A.
The wilderness and the city.
Includes bibliographical references and index.
1. Philosophy, American—20th century. I. Title.
B935.W44   191   82 — 4769
ISBN 0 — 87023 — 375 — 0   AACR2

To Grace,

who taught me the inward tolerance of life
and the inner check

Contents

The way of reflection is long. The forest of our common human ignorance is dark and tangled. Happy indeed are those who are content to live and to work only in regions where the practical labors of civilization have cleared the land, and where the task of life is to till the fertile fields and to walk in the established ways. The philosopher, in the world of thought, is by destiny forever a frontiersman. To others he must often seem the mere wanderer. He knows best himself how far he wanders, and how often he seems to be discovering only new barrenness in the lonely wilderness—Josiah Royce, 1900

The frontiersman may wander; but he must some day win what shall belong to the united empire of human truth. Those are wrong who ask him merely to stay at home. He wanders because he must; and God is to be found also in the wildernesses and in the solitary places of thought. But those are right who ask that the student of philosophy shall find, if he succeeds at all, a living truth; and that the God of the wilderness, if indeed he be the true God, shall show himself also as the keeper of the city.—Josiah Royce, 1900

I do not expect to see in my day a genuine, as distinct from a forced and artificial, integration of thought. But a mind that is not too egotistically impatient can have faith that this unification will issue in its season. Meantime a chief task of those who call themselves philosophers is to help get rid of the useless lumber that blocks our highways of thought, and to strive to make straight and open the paths that lead to the future. Forty years spent in wandering in a wilderness like that of the present is not a sad fate—unless one attempts to make himself believe that the wilderness is after all itself the promised land.—John Dewey, 1930

Preface

The following study is the result of an inquest into the thought of
Josiah Royce, C. S. Peirce, William James, John Dewey, and George
Santayana, who are widely acknowledged to be the great American classical philosophers. The purpose of my inquiry and of this
report of its results has been to determine what is still vital, in the
sense of true to life, in the American philosophical tradition; what
can be brought forward from it into our own time as the foundation for a contemporary philosophy of life. My discussion, then,
does not take the form of a standard commentary, but is, in the
sense of Alfred North Whitehead, a "recurrence" to the great
American thinkers, an attempt to make contact with their spirit, to
bring into the foreground some themes that have been neglected
by most of their successors, to make them live as serious thinkers
grappling with fundamental human predicaments, and to draw
vitality from them. I am engaging in "interpretation" as Josiah
Royce defined it. We are, according to Royce, sources of ideas for
one another; we define ourselves through "contrast effects" with
others. In my own speculative work, which I consider to be deeply
within the American tradition, I define the core of personality as
the expression of others to oneself. I have here tried to express the
great American thinkers to myself accurately, sympathetically,
and critically. I have tried to make my interpretation "representative" in the sense of classical criticism; not merely mine, but gener-

ally relevant to the American mind and helpful for those who seek to understand that mind.

Despite differences in terminology and even in positions on specific issues, the great American philosophers share a deep unity of thought which places them within a single universe of discourse and allows one to speak correctly of an American tradition of philosophy. The term "American" in this case may appear to be deceptive, because Royce, Peirce, James, Dewey, and Santayana were New England philosophers by birth, upbringing, or place of working life. American philosophy, then, is a growth of New England, but it has been appropriated more or less adequately by the rest of the country as the United States became a nation and, perhaps, by now an empire. The core of the New England mind is puritan, and the great American philosophers interpret the modern spirit through puritan categories or, in Santayana's case, in explicit reaction to them. I have attempted in the light of John Dewey's method to separate the "adventitious" aspects of puritanism from its universal contribution, and to show how that contribution might inform a contemporary philosophy of life. Of course, I do not claim that what is universal from my viewpoint might not be adventitious from another's, or the reverse. The best that a speculative philosopher can do is to put forward an appeal as genuinely and rigorously as possible and hope that it is sufficiently inviting to generate vigorous discussion.

The hallmark of the American philosophical tradition, from the perspective developed here, is that existential perplexities, particularly the determination of fundamental commitments by the individual, should be resolved morally. The puritan mind is viewed here primarily as a moral mind, which at its best, in the profound expressions of the great American philosophers, penetrates to the deepest structures of the moral outlook. The most fundamental of those structures is what James called "inner tolerance" or what the critic Irving Babbitt called "the inner check." In order to be moral, for the American thinkers, one must be able to tolerate life in its fullness, the evil as well as the good. One must keep steady in one's vision the totality of experience and still commit oneself to some form of service to others. I hold, then, that American philosophy is not a form of "cheap optimism" as Karl Jaspers called it in *Man in the Modern Age*. Rather, the puritan contribution to philosophy of life is the deepening and clarifying of tenacity into a sublime virtue of toleration. The strength and brute persistence of tenacity is transformed by the great American philosophers into a steady resolve to promote goodness despite all of the ontological considerations, particularly finitude and contingency, which might lead to slackness of will, the spiritual disease of *acedia*. Often what I consider to be the essential American contribution to philosophy is obscured by appeals to devotion to the community that are not backed by serious reflection on the difficulties in the way of such dedication. I have judged these appeals to be "adventitious," in Dewey's sense, and have critiqued them, I trust, in his spirit.

The thought of the great American philosophers may be fruitfully understood as a response to the fin-de-siècle pessimism and decadence, to the feeling or idea that one is justified in giving up on existence, in letting oneself go either by submergence into a narrow and militant enthusiasm, or by purposeless hedonic indulgence. Similar tendencies are surfacing in contemporary American life, as the twentieth century draws to a close, and the best antidote to them is a revitalization of our tradition. The American classical philosophers counseled a difficult discipline combining harsh self-control and the broadest and deepest sympathy. It is just such virtue that at least should be more widely understood today. A revulsion against "permissiveness" is building in the middle classes today. Unless the demand for social control is tempered by self-control and by sympathy on the parts of the privileged who make the demand, America may be in for a bitter and brutal era of reaction. Although the following study is a discussion of philosophy of life and not of politics and history, it should be read with the contemporary public situation and the puritan tradition in mind. We need, I believe, to recover the best elements of that tradition, and philosophy is one domain in which that recovery might begin.

In designing and executing the following work I was aided by Deena Weinstein, who helped me to formulate the project in the first instance, discussed each chapter with me thoroughly before it was written, and critiqued the resulting drafts of each chapter with acuity. Frederic Homer, John Lachs, and Richard McDermott commented constructively on the manuscript, enabling me to make substantial improvements in the discussion. Richard Martin of the University of Massachusetts Press provided intelligent and sympathetic care for the manuscript throughout the editorial process. Pam Campbell was a skillful and perceptive copy editor, and Richard Hiner gave ready editorial assistance on references. The University of Wyoming, by awarding me the Milward Simpson Professorship in Political Science in 1979, offered me the time and congenial environment to work on the manuscript, as did Purdue University through its grant of a Humanities Fellowship in 1981. The staff of the Newberry Library in Chicago, Illinois, particularly Karen Skubish who granted me carrel space there, provided a fine environment for completing the final version of the manuscript.

West Lafayette, Indiana, 1981

1

American Philosophy as a Form of Modern Philosophy

The essence of modern philosophy is the expression of an image of human existence and of its major possibilities that appeals to the free judgment of individuals. Philosophy in the modern period is an effort to provide an answer to the question that George Santayana posed in *Dominations and Powers:* "What will liberty bring to the free man?" Santayana believed that this query was the "great question of morals and politics." He was correct, at least, for the modern period, in which the creation of free individuals became the supreme justification of conduct. The modern period was initiated intellectually when René Descartes sought to gain new foundations for knowledge by separating himself from tradition, though only provisionally, and by making himself his object of study. Modern thought, then, was initiated by an act of radical separation of the thinker from the social and cultural world. The two significant moments of modern philosophy that have occurred in the centuries succeeding Descartes, that of Immanuel Kant and that of Friedrich Nietzsche, have deepened the separation of individual from world by giving it first a moral and then an existential dimension. In brief sketch, the "thinking substance" of Descartes became the moral subject of Kant, which in turn was transformed into the vital will of Nietzsche. In each case the separateness of the individual from that which is not its own was the founding act of thought about human concerns. In order to be modern it is necessary to make oneself separate from one's environs.

The quality of the separation, what one makes one's object in the state of separateness, determines the quality of individuality. There is no modernity without individuals who actually affirm themselves and without images of possible individuality. The intellectual climate of today is unfavorable to individualism and emphasizes the priority of biological, social, and cultural conditions rather than the intimate and personal center of expression and decision which is the core of each human being. There is no way in which it can be demonstrated that individuality is superior to any of the other possible claims on human conduct, because any such attempt at demonstration would defeat itself by subordinating the free judgment, which is the basis of individuality, to a standard regulative over it. Freedom, which is of, by, and for individuals, is self-justifying or it is not justified at all. That is why Santayana's query does not seek the meaning of freedom, but the objects and understandings that might have a claim upon it. Modern philosophers offer appeals to the free judgment, not revelations or compulsions. Free judgment is one of the existential consequences of radical separation. If human beings do not find it possible to separate themselves from their involvements with others and to take a stand of their own toward their lives there can be no individuals. Modern philosophy is a story of how to be an individual. Each modern philosopher or group of modern philosophers who share common terms of discourse adds to that story and reinterprets the tales previously told.

The ability of human beings to separate themselves in thought, feeling, and will from their attachments to the world, particularly the social world, creates the problem of how union should be restored. Those who withdraw to take an independent stand toward their lives may formulate judgments that are opposed to the dominant hierarchies of importance. Descartes was so aware of and frightened by this possibility that he set up a provisional morality for himself, which emphasized obedience to custom and to constituted authority, while he undertook his speculative researches. The philosophers who succeeded Descartes attempted to work out more durable solutions to the problem of relating the freely critical self to collective life. None of these proposed solutions, insofar as they impaired free judgment, was successful. A voluntary community of individuals is the only way in which the separate self can satisfactorily achieve relation with other human beings, but such a community is merely an ideal. The limitations placed on free judgment by modern philosophers, their suggestions about what liberty should bring to free individuals, are ways of providing content to community and of restoring the union that has been broken by radical separation. The images of human existence and of its possibilities created by modern philosophers show how each particular thinker or group of thinkers understood radical separation and achieved reunion with other persons and perhaps with the cosmos. Modern philosophy is intensely personal, because it is a record of how particular individuals formed their life-commitments, but it is also representative, because philosophers offer their own life-commitments as models for others to evaluate and criticize, and, perhaps, to embrace and emulate.

Modern philosophy, then, is formed by a dialectic, the first moment of which is the unselfconscious unity of the self and the world, including other selves; the second moment of which is the radical separation of the self from that which is not its own; and the third moment of which is the reunion, on the basis of a design that preserves some independence for the self, of the self with that which is other than itself. The abstract dialectic is given content by the doubts that appear and the questions that are raised when philosophers take up a stance of radical separation. Josiah Royce compared his experience of radical separation to wandering alone in a wilderness. His aim was to find in the wilderness of doubt the insight into the true commitment to the practical life of the city. Thus, Royce evinces the double movement of modern philosophy and of individuality, which involves separation in order to criticize and reunion in order to affirm. If both moments are not present and are not repeated continually, then the experienced or vital tension, which is necessary to maintain individuality, is broken. In the absence of tension the self may become so detached that it falls into despair or *acedia*, or the self may become so committed that it becomes a mere part of a "crowd" or a "herd," and, thus, subject to external direction. The free individual must be close enough to other people to affirm a common life with them and to participate in the affairs of the world, and distant enough from them to be critical of loyalties.

American philosophy is a variant or a branch of modern philosophy and, therefore, is structured by the modern dialectic. American philosophers journeyed into the wilderness with their doubts and offered their images of human existence and its possibilities to those who remained within the city. The following discussion is an interpretation of the great American philosophers, Josiah Royce, C. S. Peirce, William James, John Dewey, and George Santayana. These thinkers have been called by Andrew Reck the "classic American philosophers."[1] They will be referred to here as the "American classical philosophers." The term "modern classical philosophy" was coined by Benjamin K. Rand, a Harvard colleague of Royce, James, and Santayana, to refer to the "chief philosophical systems" created by the "great philosophers" of the present era.[2] American classical philosophy refers to the chief philosophical systems created by the great American thinkers. It is, of course, impossible to give a precise definition of great philosophy, because each system of philosophical ideas has its own interpretation of greatness. The five thinkers discussed here were chosen from the many other American philosophers because of the widespread agreement with Reck's judgment that they are, indeed, the "classic" figures; the cultural importance and centrality which the consensus indicates; and the seriousness and thoroughness of reflection of these figures which make the consensus appropriate. The American classical philosophers, when considered as a group, provide a distinctive response to the challenge of defining what liberty should mean to free people. The following discussion is an effort to evaluate their contribution to life-philosophy and, especially, to determine what, if anything, is still relevant within it, by which is meant, what is still true to life. The term "life-philosophy" is used here to refer to thought that seeks to provide an interpretation of conduct and its environing context, and particularly of the basic commitments of the individual to the world and to others. Life-philosophy is the capstone of the modern philosophical tradition; the essence of modern classical philosophy is life-philosophy.

The organizing images through which American life-philosophy is interpreted in the present work are "wilderness" and "city." These dialectically opposed and yet reciprocal terms are, as was noted above, drawn from the thought of Josiah Royce, who used them to clarify the philosopher's vocation. For Royce, "wilderness" was the mental space into which the philosopher withdrew in an act of separation from the moral conventions, the cognitive assumptions, and the practical certitudes of the "city." In Royce's lexicon, as in the terms of the present work, the idea of "city" is straightforward and readily definable as the everyday social life of human beings in their actual communities. The "God of the city," to which Royce refers, is the guarantor of the community's norms and assumptions. In contrast to the term "city," that of "wilderness" is flexible and open-ended. Few human beings choose or are impelled to suspend judgment on the validity of the city's judgments and thereby to separate themselves from their communities. Those who do enter the free mental space of the wilderness may find there any number of different objects and states of being. For Royce the journey into the wilderness was an attempt to doubt the received certitudes of the city, not in order to break them down, but to discover and to think through a more rational basis for them and, therefore, to strengthen the bonds of community by giving them self-conscious justification. The philosopher would demonstrate, according to Royce, that the "God of the wilderness," that of the individual and separated self, is one and the same as the "God of the city." Not all individuals who enter the wilderness, however, will find a treasure there that will allow them to reenter the community with a special gift. They may not encounter any god there and may suffer instead the despair described by such modern existentialists as Sören Kierkegaard and Miguel de Unamuno. But all those who enter the wilderness will come there with doubt. The wilderness is most fundamentally a place of doubting.

What the wilderness means for individuals who enter it will depend on what and how they doubt. Royce undertook a regimen of methodical doubting after the manner of Descartes and ended by questioning the existence of a world beyond the contents revealed in a single span of attention. William James carried doubting far more deeply and not only wondered why there should be a world of experience rather than no world at all, but touched the concrete root of doubting, the panic fear that one's own personal existence will lose its integrity. James, of all the American classical philosophers, explored the wilderness devoid of God most thoroughly. He intensified the doubt and the unsettled frame of mind that most generally define the journey into the wilderness and transmuted

them into agonized self-searching terminating in the encounter
with nothingness. James, then, is the American classical philosopher who desublimates the methodical doubting of Royce and the
lived doubting about particular beliefs of C. S. Peirce. It is the
Jamesian gaze at the wilderness, which espies Nietzsche's abyss,
that defines the term "wilderness" most radically in the present
study. Royce's methodical doubting separated him from the life of
the city only provisionally. From the standpoint of a wilderness in
which no god appears Royce must have taken many of the bless-
ings of the city with him into the wilderness. But existentialists for
whom the abyss has replaced God can only speak for their own
experience. The insight resulting in a vision of a strip of personal
experience surrounded by vacancy is the key that deciphers the
following critical commentary on the American classical philosophers. My own wilderness and James's are very similar, which is
why the turning point of the commentary comes at the middle of
the chapter on James, which is the middle chapter of the study. A
journey into the Jamesian wilderness sets the individual distinctly
over against the community, because it brings out the discrete and
inalienable elements of personal experience, the heightening of
individuality against the background of vacancy. James overcame
separation from the community only by turning his back on the
wilderness into which he had been thrown by positing himself as
a moral actor through a heroic act of will and determination. His
"will to believe," however, is only one way of responding to the
godless wilderness, as Nietzsche's project of self-overcoming and
Heidegger's quest after Being demonstrate.

One of the primary contributions of the city to individuals is its
provision of reasons and motivations to live, particularly to live fully in active service to others. One of the consequences of a journey
into the Jamesian or godless wilderness may be an individual's
loss of any zest for living or vivacity, of any urge or will to transcend
the self through participation in cooperative activities. Throughout the following discussion, the term *acedia* will be used to refer
to the state of being that James called "world sickness," in which
the self succumbs to hatred of its own existence and in which experience is felt at best as dull, flat, and boring, and at worst as utterly repulsive and repugnant. The term *acedia* is used in the present study as Irving Babbitt, the American critic and contemporary
of the philosophers treated here, defined it. For Babbitt, who

delineated more clearly than any other American thinker the grounds of a self-critical individualism, *acedia* in modern times is marked by a sense of loneliness, forlornness, and solitude that crushes the will to strive. *Acedia* is the state of being of an individual who has become separated from involvement with the common life and who either cannot or will not find a way back to such involvement, though the separation is acutely painful. The contemporary American theologian Martin E. Marty, whose *Varieties of Unbelief* parallels James's *Varieties of Religious Experience*, defines *acedia* as "paralysis, or listlessness, in the face of potentially good acts or beliefs": "The man of God is made for joy but turns away. The man approached by the philosopher of value may be bored. When medieval theologians spoke of this capital sin, they did not refer to the mere laziness implied in the modern translation, 'sloth.' They meant the canceling-out of seriousness."[3] For Marty, *acedia* is the negation of receptivity to God's grace and should be counteracted by awakening such receptivity. For those who find the abyss in the wilderness, *acedia* is to be overcome by a leap of commitment such as James defended or by a slow assimilation of the hatred for existence that underlies it such as Nietzsche counseled but could not himself accomplish.

In his discussion of "The Human Religiousness of William James" William A. Clebsch has defined James's spiritual crisis of 1868 – 1872 as an encounter with *acedia*. In James's case *acedia* took the form of "a bleak, suicidal depression attended by insomnia, eye trouble, weakness of the back, and digestive disorders," and marked by "long bouts of disdain for life" which were "briefly punctuated—and aggravated—by a few flashes of euphoria." In 1870, Clebsch comments, James suffered "a deep crisis of dire disgust with his own existence, culminating in a downhill plunge of vital energy, of the will to live." Only when James cracked through the anaesthetic and protective surface of *acedia*, and felt the "panic fear" supervening on a glimpse at the "pit of insecurity beneath the surface of life," was the way prepared for him to affirm life in the face of dread. Clebsch notes that *acedia* is related to "overscrupulous wondering about what one ought to do" which tempts "one to suicide as the only escape from the ennui and the guilt of inactivity: . . . Victims of acedia could love nothing, could hate themselves only for their inability to love anything, including themselves."[4] The connection of *acedia* with doubt places this state of being in the "wilderness." It is, indeed, the normal state of being in the wilderness, the way in which the vivid and acute despair of panic fear over the flimsiness of the tissue of one's personal experience is muted and anaesthetized. Just as the state of nature for Thomas Hobbes was a state of war, not because it was marked by continuous physical conflict, but because it was suffused by fear of violent death, so the wilderness is at its core a state of war against oneself, not because it forces one to commit suicide, but because the *acedia* that often permeates it thinly conceals the panic fear of personal dissolution.

Although it was James who penetrated deepest into the wilderness and gave detailed reports of "world sickness," Royce, in his treatment of the "wilderness," shows that he understood something of *acedia*. He remarks that the "way of reflection is long" and that "the forest of our common human ignorance is dark and tangled." Then he concludes that the philosopher "knows best himself how far he wanders, and how often he seems to be discovering only new barrenness in the lonely wilderness." Royce, however, held that though the philosopher as "frontiersman" may wander, "he must some day win what shall belong to the united empire of human truth."[5] It is, perhaps, that "must," which Royce carried with him into the wilderness, that ensured that he would find there a "soul-stirring vision of the truth" and that he would not plunge so deeply into the loneliness of *acedia* that he would find no speculative bridge back to the city. The other American classical philosophers touch on *acedia* primarily in their strictures against what they consider to be contrived and meretricious doubting. It is a thesis of the present study that Dewey and Santayana are philosophers of the city, who try to avoid the wilderness that James had found to be empty of God. Peirce who, like Dewey and Santayana, claims to work within the context of "common sense," mounts his most severe polemics against the "feigned doubting" of Descartes which he believes distracts individuals from concern with concrete good and isolates them from their fellow beings. Peirce, Dewey, and Santayana may be interpreted in the context of the following discussion as trying to forestall *acedia* by their critiques of methodical doubting. Dewey, indeed, pushes his critique to include those who "are preoccupied with the state of their character, concerned for the purity of their motives and the goodness of their souls: . . . The exaltation of conceit which sometimes accompanies this absorption can produce a corrosive inhumanity which exceeds the possibilities of any other known form of selfishness. In other cases, persistent preoccupation with the thought of an ideal realm breeds morbid discontent with surroundings, or induces a futile withdrawal into an inner world where all facts are fair to the eye."[6] Dewey's "corrosive inhumanity" and "morbid discontent with surroundings" are clearly features of *acedia* as it has been described here.

That the journey into the wilderness involves the danger of *acedia*, particularly if the wanderer does not find God there, but instead stumbles upon the abyss, is one side of the general problem of individualism in the modern world. A "sound individualism," to use the term of Irving Babbitt, for the contemporary world should be one based on an encounter with the godless wilderness and an "inner tolerance," as James called it, of the hatred for existence that arises from such an encounter. A mature and self-critical individualism, which profits from James's report of his crisis but which does not depend on exercise of the will to believe, affirms conscious life and experience as intrinsically good while remaining keenly aware of the inherent defects and flaws of such finite life. One may come to love the conscious life that is oneself and to cherish the conscious lives of others without diminishing one's hatred of death, disease, cruelty, and suffering. That, at least, whether or not it is attainable in our world, is a requirement of a reflective individualism shadowed by the death of God. But overcoming *acedia* without turning one's back on its revelations about life grasped from the inside is not the only and, perhaps, not the most important requirement of a mature individualism. Each of the American classical philosophers concluded that the greatest threat to the individual in the modern world is fanaticism, the spirit that obliterates despair by enthusiastic and single-minded imposition of a parochial ideal on nature and on other selves.

Whereas *acedia* is a retreat from involvement in life, fanaticism or, as Babbitt most precisely termed it, "efficient megalomania" is a desperate attempt to master life, to pretend that its inherent defects are but accidents. Such an attempt is doomed to failure, but will continue to be undertaken as long as modern human beings remain, in Royce's term, "viciously naive" about their limitations. All the American philosophers believed that human beings tended to deceive themselves about the limits of their existence.

Royce and Santayana held that the conscious individual has an essential tendency to make impossible demands on the world for satisfaction. Peirce, James, and Dewey taught that human beings spontaneously believed what superficially pleased them and had to learn to distinguish fact from fantasy. The adult who clings to wish fulfillment is ripe for fanaticism, which disregards the claims for individual integrity in the mad rush to evade the consequences of disillusionment about life's possibilities. Just as inner tolerance of life is the antidote for *acedia*, so what Babbitt called the "inner check" on "expansive emotion" is the prescribed cure for fanaticism, and, thus, the second requirement of reflective individualism. Both the depression of *acedia* and the mania of fanaticism are met by a "sound individualism" with the cultivation of personal virtue that tolerates self and respects the otherness of the other person.

The organizing images of wilderness and city are meant to provide a pictorial representation of the dialectical movement characterizing American life-philosophy in its response to the "death of God" problematic. Both *acedia* and fanaticism are ultimately related to the eclipse of Royce's aspiration that the God of the wilderness be revealed to be the guarantor of the city. *Acedia* occurs when one loses the taste for a flawed and finite life, whereas fanaticism arises when one attempts to take on for oneself what was once God's providential role. Although only Royce systematically developed the imagery of wilderness and city, his metaphorical description of the philosopher's vocation is appropriate to the thought of the other American classical philosophers. Each one can be understood generally within the context of that imagery: Royce and Peirce still find a beneficent God in the wilderness, James finds a "pit of insecurity" there, and Dewey and Santayana remain within the confines of the city, attempting to show how its life can be made better. For the present commentary, it is necessary to return to James's wilderness, even if it be the mental equivalent of a chemical dump or the South Bronx, a postcivilized wilderness, and to cultivate inner tolerance as a guarantor of the individual's persistence and as a ground for the inner check that preserves civility.

The question may arise of why it is particularly significant to examine the American philosophical heritage today, rather than some other tradition. I have chosen to discuss the American classical philosophers because I am, as a social being, primarily a product of American culture. Although the modern concern for the free individual is at the root of all the national traditions of philosophy in the West, each one of these traditions offers a different way of interpreting and defining the proper objects of free judgment and decision. One can be and, indeed, must be modern (if one would be modern) in some special way. José Ortega y Gasset claimed that the individual is a relation between self and circumstances. Among the most important circumstances, in the sense of those that form the content of personal character, are the orientations toward life that are dominant in one's culture. These orientations are originally acquired, without any knowledge of their relativity, by children. Philosophers, who are the quintessential adults, separate themselves from common opinion, reflect upon the prevailing orientations toward life, and crystallize and critique them. If one wishes to become aware of oneself as a social being, then, one must recur to the great philosophers of one's own culture, if, indeed, one is fortunate enough to have been nurtured in a culture that permits, or at one time has permitted, great philosophers to work. Contemporary Americans are fortunate to be heirs to a tradition of classical philosophy. At least at one time in American history (approximately in the fifty years between 1880 and 1930), American culture achieved the requisite balance between sophistication and coherence to foster an impressive national tradition in philosophy. That tradition defined some of the best possibilities of the modern spirit, and they were possibilities that were appropriate to American orientations toward life. The legacy of the American classical philosophers is a rich one which can be claimed by Americans who seek to know themselves and to carry on the modern project of forming a "sound individualism."

Whether or not the modern project should be continued is an issue for what Marvin Farber called "standpoint commitment." The general trend of current intellectual and social life is toward some form of collectivism, whether Marxist or corporatist. The reasons for this trend, which include the complexity and interdependence of contemporary economic life, and, especially, the pervasive fear engendered by weapons of mass annihilation, the destructive consequences of industrialism, the loss of traditional religious consolations, and broad resentment against life itself, are not the subjects of the present inquiry. From the modern point of view, collectivism, by which is meant here the denial of the possibility or the moral validity of the radical separation of the self for the purpose of the free criticism of life, is a reactionary position or, as the Spanish philosopher Julian Marías has called it, a form of "archaism." The appeal to the free judgment is only radical and complete when it is undertaken in a society in which the last words that people have to say about their orientations toward life have some consequence for how they conduct that life. In the present historical period there are no existing societies that permit anything close to a union of free judgment and free commitment, including, of course, American society, which drifts further and further toward a predatory corporatism. The modern project has, from its inception, been a project to be realized and never a project accomplished. From a social perspective, its essence is the cultivation of freedom from fear, which means the creation of a society that loses the character of a herd or a crowd; a society that is composed of individuals who do not panic easily and, thus, do not stampede. Such a society, it should be clear, would not require private corporate enterprise or centralized state enterprise, which Pitirim Sorokin called "decentralized totalitarianism" and "centralized capitalism," respectively. But the present inquiry is not concerned directly with social organization, although the ideal of a free society is part of the background to thought that informs it. It is concerned, rather, with some of the ways in which human beings today, specifically in America, might image their existence to themselves. The spirit of modern philosophy, as defined here, does not permit the definition of specific programs, but it requires that a mirror be held up before ourselves so that we may see better who we are and who we might be.

The present inquiry is based upon an affirmation of the modern spirit and a will to continue it into the future. It is also based upon a judgment that in the current historical period the best way in which the modern spirit can be nurtured intellectually is through a recovery of national traditions in philosophy. These traditions are the firmest available bulwarks against collectivist ideologies in the contemporary era, although they contain large measures of collectivism and were, in many cases, the progenitors of collectivist ideologies. National traditions in philosophy, therefore, cannot merely be continued in the form in which they are found, but should be criticized in terms of the insights of other traditions, the

modern spirit of free judgment, and the fullest range of experience, both actual and sympathetic, that the inquirer can integrate
into coherent thought. Those national traditions that, like the
American, are universalist carry their own antidote against provin-
cialism and group hatred. However, it would be a mistake to believe that a recurrence to a national tradition contained a last
word or a final analysis of human existence and its possibilities.
The last word, at least for a defender of free judgment, is said by
the individual, who journeys into the wilderness and takes up an
independent attitude toward the city. Insofar as a philosopher is
not a solipsist, and no philosopher who makes a public statement
can, in good faith, be a solipsist, there are as many last words as
there are self-critical individuals. Any appeals to specific group
loyalties are accidental, but accidentality is a constitutive feature
of human existence. In order to be fully modern it is necessary to
combine the universality of freedom with the particularity of acci-
dent. This is merely another indication that the modern spirit is
one that keeps opposites in perpetual tension and refuses either
to isolate itself as pure spirit or to become a mere part of an existent whole.

An insight into the background of modern philosophy, out of
which American classical thought emerged, is provided by a recurrence to its founding moment, the *cogito* of Descartes. Descartes's intellectual autobiography, which forms the first part of
his *Discourse on Method*, shows how radical separation is essential to modern thought. Descartes notes that he had been "nour-
ished on letters" since his childhood, and that because he had
been "given to believe that by their means a clear and certain
knowledge could be obtained of all that is useful in life" he had
"an extreme desire to acquire instruction." He reports that in pursuit of the fulfillment of his desire he completed the entire course
of study "at the close of which one is usually received into the
ranks of the learned." However, he was not satisfied that he had
achieved knowledge because he was still "embarrassed with so
many doubts and errors" that it appeared to him that instruction
had only compounded his ignorance. Thus, Descartes began his
wandering, moving beyond the prescribed course of study and
reading through all the books that he could acquire, "treating of
what is considered most curious and rare." Again he was disap-
pointed and concluded, taking the "liberty" of judging all others

by himself, that there was no "learning in the world." Descartes observes that in his various studies he learned that it is good to examine all things, "even those most full of superstition and falsehood, in order that we may know their just value, and avoid being deceived by them." However, the perfection of his judgment was small consolation for the doubt with which he continued to be plagued. Thus, as soon as he was old enough to escape from the control of his tutors, Descartes resolved "to seek no other science than that which could be found in myself, or at least in the great book of the world."[7]

Modern philosophy can be traced to Descartes's decision to leave the republic of letters and to wander through the world in search of a truth with which authority could not provide him. He began, by making this decision, the discipline of withdrawal into the wilderness of doubt that Josiah Royce considered to be the essence of philosophy. Descartes, of course, did not at first understand that his project was to search himself. He employed the rest of his youth "in travel," in "collecting" varied experiences, in testing himself against particular challenges, and in reflecting on what he underwent, so that he might "derive some profit" from his experience. However, the world of public affairs provided Descartes with no more knowledge than he had gained from academic studies. After much wandering he concluded that there was nothing in the manners of other people to give him "settled convictions," and that the lesson of his search had been "to believe nothing too certainly of which I had only been convinced by example and custom." Yet Descartes retained his "excessive desire to learn to distinguish the true from the false, in order to see clearly and to walk with confidence in this life."[8]

Descartes's desire "to see clearly and to walk with confidence in this life" by learning to distinguish "the true from the false" is the motive that informs modern life-philosophy. Until the twentieth century, the hope of the modern life-philosopher was that a truth existed to regulate the deliverance of the active self to the world. Descartes's account of his predicament, however, contains the presupposition, which he does not express clearly, that he is free to choose among widely varying possibilities for commitment. His "excessive desire . . . to walk with confidence" conceals from him the absoluteness of his freedom to walk down any path. In contemporary times the absolute freedom of commitment implicit in

Descartes's intellectual autobiography is made explicit in the philosophy of Jean-Paul Sartre, who, at least in his early work, tamed the desire to walk with confidence and found the truth of human existence in the individual's free judgment. Thus, he undermined the project of seeking a truth in the nature of things to regulate life-commitment and defended self-responsibility. Descartes, however, did not get behind his search for an objective truth that could give him the confidence to act. Instead he "one day formed the resolution" of making himself "an object of study" and of employing all the strength of his mind in choosing the road he should follow.

Descartes devised his method of questioning all the opinions that he held while he was "shut up alone in a stove-heated room," where he had "complete leisure" to dwell on his thoughts. He compared himself to "one who walks alone and in the twilight," and, so that he could be sure not to stumble, resolved to be circumspect in affirming any conclusions, trusting only his reason. His caution extended to a reluctance to be concerned with the affairs of the city, and he criticized "those turbulent and unrestful spirits who, being called neither by birth nor fortune to the management of public affairs, never fail to have always in their minds some new reforms."[9] Descartes insisted that his design involved trying to reform his own opinions, not social institutions or practices, and that he sought to build his thought on a foundation that was entirely his own. The Cartesian initiation of modern thought was undertaken by a separation of the self from involvement in the practical concerns of the city, but not by an opposition of the self to the forms of the city's life. Descartes's spirit of obedience to constituted authority and the character of his radical separation are made clear by the provisional morality that he adopted while he was engaged in his systematic doubting. Remarking that he could not tear down and rebuild his house of intellect unless he had a temporary dwelling in which to live, Descartes, who understood that action is exclusive and decisive, formed "a code of morals for the time being which did not consist of more than three or four maxims."

For the purposes of life-philosophy, Descartes's provisional morality is far more important to discuss than the famous *cogito* in which his method of systematic doubting resulted. The Cartesian search was for the guidance of life-commitment, for truths that would enable the individual to "walk with confidence in this life." The method of systematic doubting, however, issued merely in the judgment that one can be certain only of the existence of a thinking ego, which, implicitly, had no inherent standard for determining the proper conduct of life. The moral emptiness of the Cartesian thinking substance is matched by the concrete directives of the temporary moral code. The first of Descartes's maxims was "to obey the laws and customs of my country, adhering constantly to the religion in which by God's grace I had been instructed since my childhood." Thus, Descartes was able to overcome the doubt occasioned by the cultural relativity of morals and faiths by adopting the beliefs of his childhood, though only as a means to allow him to pursue his project of providing a firm ground for human knowledge. The second maxim, "that of being as firm and resolute in my actions as I could be, and not to follow less faithfully opinions the most dubious, when my mind was once made up regarding them, than if these had been beyond doubt," gave Descartes even greater security than his adoption of traditional faith. He was enabled by adhering to this maxim to resolve doubt concerning choices in particular situations by demanding of himself a merely formal consistency of action. Descartes was emphatic about the benefits that resulted from following his second maxim: "And henceforward this principle was sufficient to deliver me from all the penitence and remorse which usually affect the mind and agitate the conscience of those weak and vacillating creatures who allow themselves to keep changing their procedure, and practice as good, things which they afterwards judge to be evil."[10]

Descartes's first and second maxims set up his general relation to the public life of the city. He was determined to be a loyal member of society, no different outwardly from any other ordinary subject or citizen, but guided in his obedience by a new spirit. The ordinary subject or citizen kept the traditional faith and acted resolutely out of naive confidence in the absoluteness of cultural norms. The Cartesian maxims, in contrast, prescribed obedience to the prescriptions of constituted authority as means to the achievement of a speculative project. Descartes's third and fourth maxims structured his specific relation to the city's life. The third maxim, "to try always to conquer myself rather than fortune, and to alter my desires rather than change the order of the world, and

generally to accustom myself to believe that there is nothing entirely within our power but our own thoughts," is a counsel that
recalls the Stoic dicta in the *Enchiridion* of Epictetus. The *ataraxia*,
or indifference to fortune, which the Hellenistic philosophers of
conduct cultivated, is a perennial refuge of displaced spirits in
times of cultural change and of increased contact among different
social groups. Descartes, the wanderer concerned with the relativity of moral knowledge and in search of an absolute standard to
regulate life-commitment, withdrew into himself morally as a
prelude to his encounter with himself as a thinking being. His resolve to accustom himself to the belief that he had power only over
his own thoughts insured that Descartes would discover that the
essence of his existence was to think. As Nietzsche was later to
conclude, we discover our being in those domains in which we
exert power, in which subject and object are synthesized, without
being dissolved, in an act. In accordance with the restrictions built
into his provisional morality, Descartes enacted the being of
thought by making himself, as pure thinker, the object of his
power of attention. The radical separation that constitutes
modern philosophy, then, is, in its first moment, Stoical. In his
discussion of his third maxim Descartes remarked that "the long
exercise and meditation often repeated," which is required to
gain mastery over thought and to surrender concern with external
occurrences, was "the secret of those philosophers who, in ancient times, were able to free themselves from the empire of fortune, or, despite suffering or poverty, to rival their gods in their
happiness."[11]

The fourth maxim of Descartes's provisional morality followed
from the Stoical attitude toward existence that he adopted in his
third maxim. Having defined his orientation toward life, Descartes
felt that he should review "the various occupations of men in this
life in order to try to choose out the best." He decided, of course, to
devote his life to "cultivating my Reason, and in advancing myself
as much as possible in the knowledge of the truth in accordance
with the method which I had prescribed myself." His first three
maxims had created the existential and moral conditions for him
to undertake a radical separation of himself from the partial and
practical affairs of the city. His separation was meditative and depended upon a set of relations that he forged with his circumstances. Morally, the provisional code related Descartes to his cir-

cumstances as an ordinary subject or citizen. His conduct would not be any different from that of other obedient persons, though the spirit in which he obeyed would be new. Existentially, the temporary code related Descartes to his circumstances by severely limiting his expectations. In the terms of John Dewey, Descartes emphasized the "arts of acceptance," by which the self adjusts passively to the conditions in its environment, rather than the "arts of control," through which the self attempts to alter circumstances to bring them into accord with its desires. Most fundamentally, Descartes won his separation and, therefore, his individuality, by remaining passive toward the city and obedient to its God. His provisional code was comprised of an alienation of his conscience and his concrete existence to the city. He received in return for his obedience the freedom of speculative thought.

The two moments of modern thought that succeeded Descartes's initiating moment have drawn the moral and existential dimensions of the self into the ambit of radical separation. Kant's postulation of a "practical reason," against which the self could judge the moral validity of its conduct, withdrew authority over conscience from any established institution and placed it in the law-giving individual. Thus, Kant replaced the first two maxims of Descartes's provisional morality, the unquestioning obedience to traditional guides to conduct and the prudent consistency with one's resolves, with a rational conception of action. Philosophy was, therefore, enabled to gain a new foothold over the mind, and simultaneously, more of the world came under the scope of the free judgment of the individual. But the Kantian liberation of the moral self from unquestioning obedience to authority was only a partial advance. Kant followed in Descartes's path by counseling an existential attitude of prudence and by fitting between the merely technical imperatives, prescribing effective means, and the categorical imperative, concerning the form of moral conduct, an "assertorial" imperative, expressing the "practical necessity of an action as a means to the advancement of happiness."[12] For Kant, happiness should not be interpreted "as necessary for an uncertain and merely possible purpose, but for a purpose which we may presuppose with certainty and *a priori* in every man, because it belongs to his being." Happiness, according to Kant, is the one purpose which rational beings "not merely may have, but which we may with certainty assume that they all actually *have* by natural necessity." Thus, although Kant delivered moral decision to the free judgment of the individual by detaching it from specific consequences and from particular commands determined by tradition or by arbitrary will, he held his basic attitude toward life relative to an *a priori* content. In this respect, Kant was the last of the early group of modern classical philosophers, because he still adhered to the wisdom of prudence and moderation associated with the Greco-Roman philosophers of conduct, who did not separate the self from the more general environment of being.

The third moment of modern thought, the existential, completes the gathering of the world into the self by delivering to the self not only judgment over truth and right, but judgment over one's life as a whole. Existential separation is the most radical of all of the separations created in the modern era, in that it makes each individual absolutely responsible for determining a life-commitment, just because no rational grounds can be provided for any specific commitment or for even making such a commitment rather than resorting to suicide. Descartes was a liberator of scientific thought from dependence upon traditional accounts of being and customary practices. He submitted theory to the criteria of logical reason and of clear and distinct ideas. Kant similarly liberated conscience from traditional commands and specific habits by subordinating it to a formal law of practical reason that allowed for free judgment over the content of ends. The existential moment of modern thought, however, does not liberate any function or dimension of the individual from authority or specific determination of fact, but places life as a whole in the individual's charge. In the terms of Max Stirner, who was one of the first thinkers to understand and to take an existential attitude, the self is a "creative nothing" who is potentially the owner of its life. Existential separation means the withdrawal of the self from involvement in practical concerns and into "nothingness." This most concrete form of separation is best understood by considering the accounts of those who have practiced it, most notably Martin Heidegger.

Heidegger's description of essential thinking, his version of radical separation, appears in the postscript to "What is Metaphysics?" as part of a response to the objection that his philosophy "delivers all judgments regarding the truth to a chance mood" (the dread that reveals Nothingness) and, therefore, is a "Philosophy of Pure Feeling."[13] Heidegger counters this objection by noting that

"Being is not an existing quality of what-is, nor, unlike what-is, can Being be conceived and established objectively."[14] He prepares the way for a nonobjective establishment of Being by suggesting that thinkers should "make ready for one thing only: . . . to experience in Nothing the vastness of that which gives every being the warrant to be." That vastness, he claims, is "Being itself." The attitude of radical separation is, then, for Heidegger, the "making ready" to experience Being in Nothing.

Readiness for the experience of nothingness means being put in touch with a "thinking whose truth no logic can grasp," the "thoughts" of which are "absolutely determined by what is 'other' than what-is." Heidegger claims that essential thinking "answers to the demands of Being in that man surrenders his historical being to the simple, sole necessity whose constraints do not so much necessitate as create the need (Not) which is consummated in the freedom of sacrifice."[15] From this description Heidegger goes on to define the need as that of preserving the truth of being "no matter what may happen to man and everything that 'is.' " However, the definition cannot itself appear in the phenomenon of essential thinking, which makes the definition possible by disclosing the demands of Being, which latter were not known in advance of readiness. The phenomenon of essential thinking, in Heidegger's description, is exhausted by the "surrender of historical being in the freedom of sacrifice."

Heidegger's characterization of essential thinking is paradoxical, containing the notes of both surrender (necessity) and sacrifice (freedom). Indications of what he means are provided earlier in "What is Metaphysics?" by his identification of the "will to will" as "the prototype of which—'the will to power'—all appearance began." Historical being, which demands concern with objects, or "what-is," is sustained by the will to will. Concern is not automatic, as Kant believed, but depends upon an affirmation of Being, which may later be disguised by a preoccupation with limited concerns directed toward realizing particular ends. Essential thinking is a surrender of the will to will, under the impact of dread, which is not itself willed, but it is also a free sacrifice, because, for Heidegger, the essence of freedom is "letting-be." In the phenomenon of essential thinking, then, there is a surrender of the calculation of consequences with regard to particular projects and, therefore, a permission for Being to appear. Essential thinking might also be characterized as a return to the source of limited practical concern, which means not only an insight into the grounds of practicality, but much more profoundly a test of whether "being-in-the-world," the integration of self and circumstance, will be affirmed freely "no matter what may happen to man and everything that 'is,' " or whether it will be rejected resentfully because it does not conform to the collective illusions of social groups. Withstanding the test means expressing that "hidden *thanking*" which "alone does homage to the grace wherewith Being has endowed the nature of man." Such original thanking is, in Nietzsche's terms, the "overcoming" of the resentment against Being that lies at the core of all human rebellion against finitude.

Heidegger's variant of radical separation, which is perhaps the most widely discussed in contemporary philosophy, places individuals who undertake it in a position in which they must determine a basic attitude toward their own existence and that which sustains it. The dread about one's finitude, which, for Heidegger, reveals the radical contingency of existence, the character of the individual as being-toward-death, and the nothing against which all particular things stand out, is the gateway to an affirmation or a denial of "being-in-the-world." The affirmation of existence is, for Heidegger, a gratitude for Being, a hymn of thanksgiving for it which is not motivated by any benefits that the individual has received, but by the disclosure to the individual of the intrinsic "dignity" of Being. Heidegger's "original thanking" is his resolution of the predicament that arises for the individual who lives out concretely Ortega's proposition that "my life is the radical reality," that the self is the center and possessor of its own life and is free to adopt any attitude toward it on the whole. The awareness that one's life is the radical reality is made possible by setting that life against the background of nothingness. Against this background the brute factuality, contingency, and accidentality of one's life are sharply etched. The withdrawal from "everyday" commitments, which the individual ordinarily takes for granted, and the preoccupation with the character of one's existence itself, rather than with what is true or with what is right, is attended by a withering anxiety, a loss of hold on life. Out of this anxiety the individual may form a general attitude toward existence. Heidegger's attitude was to be grateful for Being and to devote himself to guarding Being from effacement by the pride of the "will to will," which reposed dignity in humanity and not in Being.

Heidegger's "fundamental ontology," the culmination of which is the attitude of thanksgiving toward Being, is not the only possible result of radical separation. The bare state of radical separation is merely the withdrawal from practical concerns and commitments, and into one's own life, which one discovers to be bordered by nothingness. The anxiety or dread that attends the state of radical separation may be overcome just as readily by an absolute posit of the finite ego, which was Max Stirner's solution; by a posit of a moral actor, such as William James undertook; or by an effort to exercise the will to power in complete awareness of the failure of finite life, as Nietzsche proposed. The most critical position that can be taken toward the state of existential separation is that it provides the basis for a thoroughgoing empiricism, what William James called a "radical empiricism." The radical separation that constitutes the existential moment of modern thought does not give, by itself, any grounds for the kind of disclosure of Being sought by Heidegger. A more critical existentialism emphasizes not "the vastness of that which gives every being the warrant to be," but the insubstantiality and the fragility of the strip of appearance that composes the content of a personal or owned life. Insubstantiality, fragility, fluency, and mobility are the hallmarks of "lived experience," as William James, the American classical philosopher whose thought drew closest to existentialism and who experienced radical separation in its most acute form, understood.

Existential separation, which gives the individual responsibility to determine an attitude toward life, is at the antipodes from the naive irresponsibility of Cartesian detachment. After he had made his decision to occupy his "whole life" in cultivating his Reason, Descartes removed himself from "all places where any acquaintances were possible" and "retired" to Holland, where, "in the crowded throng of a great and very active nation, which is more concerned with its own affairs than curious about those of others, without missing any of the conveniences of the most populous towns," he could "live as solitary and retired as in deserts most remote."[16] Having alienated his moral and his existential judgment, Descartes could "roam hither and thither, trying to be a spectator rather than an actor in all the comedies the world displays." The philosopher who is most the heir to the Cartesian legacy in contemporary thought, Jean-Paul Sartre, may be said to have roamed hither and thither trying to be an actor rather than a spectator in all the tragedies the world displays. Sartre's existential separation is far more radical than Descartes's observational detachment, but, paradoxically, it does not permit him any peace from the affairs of the city. The responsibility engendered by existential separation is responsibility for the determination of one's life as a whole, particularly for one's relations to other centers of judgment. Modern philosophy has filled in the individual to the point at which the subject of its reflections is not the thinking being or the moral subject, but the concrete person, Miguel de Unamuno's "man of flesh and bone."

Jean-Paul Sartre wrote at the end of *The Words*, his intellectual autobiography, that although "culture doesn't save anything or anyone, it doesn't justify," it is "a product of man: he projects himself into it, he recognizes himself in it; that critical mirror alone offers him his image."[17] Sartre's definition of culture is even more appropriately a description of the purpose of modern philosophy. The expression of an image of human existence and of its major possibilities, of course, has not been the avowed aim of all or even of most modern philosophers. Descartes, for example, did not believe that his thought was a projection of himself and an occasion for self-recognition, but that it was a vehicle of certain knowledge about existence. Similarly, Kant did not believe that he was holding up a mirror to himself, but that his "transcendental method" disclosed the forms of rational knowledge and the universal law of conduct for rational beings. Only the existential moment of modern philosophy reveals the meaning that was implicit in the preceding moments. The Hegelian sort of notion implied here—that the spirit develops greater understanding of itself as it criticizes its past works—is necessitated as at least a regulative principle for making the development of thought intelligible. The existential moment, indeed, may not be the last phase of modern philosophy. Some new interpretation of freedom may be devised that will contain a comprehensive critique of preceding interpretations, showing that they were aimed at some objective that was not clear and distinct to those who undertook them. If such a new interpretation is made, then the existential moment will lose its contemporary relevance and become a steppingstone to a different state of consciousness and being. At any particular point in the development of thought, however, philosophers, whatever their divergent standpoints, cannot help but believe that their universe of discourse is the purest and most critical attainable. They cannot think beyond their own thought, even if they may abstractly and correctly claim that their thought may be superseded.

The idea that the very aim of philosophy becomes clarified as the products of philosophical reflection are successively criticized holds only for a series of thinkers who attend to the same general themes. Modern philosophy, for example, is a unity because it is constituted by the theme of the self as an object of study, which was sounded first by Descartes. If thinkers who call themselves "philosophers" do not make this theme central to their reflections, modern philosophy will not have reached a new stage in its development but will have been abandoned. There is no historical reason why modern philosophy must be continued into the future or even why human beings must think of themselves as individuals separate from one another. The Hegelian thesis of successive reinterpretations suggested here does not imply that the chain of critical reflection will gain more and more links. The chain, indeed, can be broken for any number of reasons that are extrinsic to the dynamics of thought, such as wars, changes in social relations, new technologies, or natural occurrences not initiated by human beings. Between the orthodox Hegelian position that "reason rules the world," and the atomistic view that each philosophical discourse is merely an internal unity, is the view that there are movements of thought in which themes are progressively clarified through the exploration of their alternative statements and their applications to the various dimensions of life. Of course, the very idea that one cannot demonstrate that reason rules the world is an insight of the existential moment of modern philosophy and is a basic principle of the systems rooted in that moment.

Sartre's thesis that culture is a "critical mirror" that offers human beings their image implies both that images are subject to the free judgment of individuals and that there are some criteria for evaluating them. The question arises, then, of what standards may be used to evaluate images that will be consistent with or will not impair free judgment. From one viewpoint, which is ultimate and definitive over all, there are no standards that can be regulative over the free judgment of each individual and still preserve the freedom of that judgment. Every standard proposed for regulating the free judgment is subject to that judgment. This only means that the last word must be a free word. There are, of course, many words to be said before the last one, and what they are and how to say them are among the most important tasks of philosophers. Each image of human existence contains its own criteria for evaluating itself and for evaluating all other images. The appeal of an image to self-knowledge and to the guidance of conduct is primarily a function of the union of its specific content with the standards by which it judges whether or not that content is adequate.

The problem of how to appeal to the free judgment appropriately is connected to Santayana's question—"What will liberty bring to the free man?"—which was raised at the outset of the present discussion. For traditional rationalist philosophies the free judgment was subordinated to reason, which provided it with principles for determining life-commitments and for guiding their implementation. For traditional empiricism, in contrast, the free judgment was submitted to feeling, in particular pleasure and pain. In the present discussion the primary criterion of appeal to the free judgment is adequacy of vision. By an adequate vision is meant one that is based on a thorough examination of a wide range of experiences, both direct and imaginative, and one that is constructed by a coherent reflection of those experiences undertaken with the aim of ordering them in a hierarchy of significance. Adequacy of vision contains both rational and empirical components. The empirical aspect, the survey of experience, is given form by the rational norm of comprehensiveness, while the rational aspect, the ordering into a coherent hierarchy, is given content by the sense of importance or significance. A vision of human existence and its possibilities should be as complete as the philosopher can make it, should put disparate experiences into coherent relations (which may include opposition or contradiction) with one another, and should give emphasis to those experiences that are most significant. Significance here refers to the character of some experiences that permits them to reveal the structure of life better than others. The most basic appeal to the free judgment made by an existential philosopher is to a sense of importance or, perhaps even more accurately, to a sense of seriousness. Those experiences that best reveal the structure of life are, for the existential philosopher, those that are stamped with seriousness. The arousal of a sense of seriousness and then the clarification, criticism, and sharpening of that sense is the basic project of an existential philosopher.

The preoccupation of existentialists with "nothingness," "dread," "responsibility," and other such terms reflects the emphasis that they place on the serious aspects of existence as keys to the interpretation of its other phases. Sartre exemplifies the type of sense of importance that constitutes existential thought, although his is a particular variant, when, in *The Words*, he writes: "Though I am now disillusioned I cannot think about the cooling of the sun without fear. I don't mind if my fellowmen forget about me the day after I'm buried. As long as they're alive, I'll haunt them, unnamed, imperceptible, present in every one of them just as the billions of dead who are unknown to me and whom I preserve from annihilation are present in me. But if mankind disappears, it will kill its dead for good."[18] Sartre, who claims that he "collared the Holy Ghost in the cellar and threw him out," and that he carried through the "cruel and long-range affair" of atheism, presents here a comprehensive and intense vision of human existence that matches in its power the visions of mystics. The humanism that Sartre expresses in his vision is what William James called the "over-belief" that guides his commitments and his basic orientation toward life. Sartre's humanism is but one possible result of a serious reflection on a wide range of experiences. The vision originates in Sartre's doubts about immortality and, in general, about the power of the spirit to effect changes in the world, and resolves that doubt in an inversion of Christian ideas of the communion of saints. His thought, then, is religious in the broadest sense of that term, in that it is concerned with final commitments and illuminates those commitments with the aid of a vision. Sartre's atheistic project, like Heidegger's effort to make a "clearing for Being" to disclose itself, are philosophical efforts to interpret the death of God and to affirm life under the shadow of that death. In greatest measure, the seriousness of existential philosophy is a function of its preoccupation with the death of God, which accounts for its dual emphases on freedom and nothingness. The free judgment is most sharply etched against the background of nothingness. It is against this background that it appears as what Nikolai Berdyaev called "meonic freedom," the nonobjective antithesis to "things." The "nausea" that Sartre describes as attending viscous Being is, in part, a response to the absence of any direction for or purpose to "meonic freedom." His fear about the cooling of the sun and his image of a humanity in which all souls penetrate into each soul are the directions that he has provided for his freedom.

The existential moment of modern thought did not occur abruptly in Western culture but was preceded by a long transitional period in which philosophers, particularly in Germany, attempted to trace the implications of Kant's idea of an autonomous practical reason. Much of nineteenth-century philosophy was devoted to trying to show that the moral law could be given a concrete historical interpretation, that reality was rational in the sense that there was an immanent historical progress toward the fulfillment of the moral will. Concurrent with the quest for a concrete universal, which is associated with Hegel's absolute idealism, was an opposing movement, which was initiated by Schopenhauer and which emphasized the irrationality of the vital will, or the "will to live." According to Schopenhauer, it is impossible to find a ground for one's volitions because "man's will is his authentic self, the true core of his being; hence it constitutes the ground of his consciousness as something which is simply given and present and beyond which he cannot go."[19] The two concurrent and opposing movements of German idealism, Hegel's absolute idealism and Schopenhauer's voluntarism, created the intellectual context in which American classical philosophy emerged. In the terms of Josiah Royce's metaphor of the city and the wilderness, Hegel's God was that of the city and Schopenhauer's that of the wilderness. Hegel gave nineteenth-century philosophy a moral bias and Schopenhauer provided it with a vital bias.

Schopenhauer was the first self-conscious life-philosopher in the West. For him, philosophy was primarily devoted to interpreting the structure of life, as it is grasped from the inside by a conscious individual, and to recommending commitments or fundamental attitudes toward life based upon his interpretation. Schopenhauer's interpretation of life was formed by a discussion of the modes of the "will to live," which included self-assertion and resignation. Schopenhauer is, of course, most widely known for his "pessimism," which was based on his belief that the will to live is insatiable and that the individuated organism is a mere means to its continuance. However, for American philosophers, most notably Josiah Royce and George Santayana, Schopenhauer's emphases upon will and life were philosophical points of departure. Royce noted in *The Problem of Christianity* that he was far more Schopenhauer's legatee than Hegel's, and that his variant of absolute idealism was most appropriately termed "absolute voluntarism." Similarly, Santayana acknowledged indebtedness to Schopenhauer, particularly for his category of "primal will," the dynamic element in nature. Royce self-consciously attempted to overcome Schopenhauer's dualism between the blind assertive will and the reflective and sublimated resigned will, while Santayana returned to Schopenhauer's dualism and refined it. The responses to Royce made by the three great pragmatists, C. S. Peirce, William James, and John Dewey, also involved, of course, interpretations of life and were structured by an underlying dialectic of the will.

In Europe, life-philosophy was developed in the late nineteenth century by such thinkers as Henri Bergson, who William James acknowledged to be a kindred spirit, and Wilhelm Dilthey, Georg Simmel, and Miguel de Unamuno, among many others. Often the irrationalism that was so prominent in Schopenhauer's thought was tempered by Hegelian historicism, as it was in Dilthey's thought, or by Kantian formalism, as it was in Simmel's life-philosophy. The American classical philosophers were members of the two generations associated in Europe with the names of Dilthey, Bergson, and Edmund Husserl. They were, at least in great part, life-philosophers, in the sense that they attempted to provide interpretations of life as it is undergone by individuated organisms, and to recommend commitments based upon their interpretations. The resources on which the American classical philosophers drew were as rich as those of their European contemporaries and included, as most important, Kantian transcendental criticism, Hegelian historicism, British and French positivism, vitalist intuitionism, and their own Calvinist religious heritage. The varied mix of influences was combined by each American classical thinker, with original additions, into a coherent image of human existence and its possibilities. Taken together, the images constructed by the American classical philosophers comprise a universe of discourse that fills out the alternatives of a general philosophy of life.

The special concern of American life-philosophy, which differentiates it, at least in accent, from the European thought of the same period, is the problem of integrating the radically separate individual into the ongoing life of the community. By pursuing this concern thoroughly and courageously the American classical thinkers encountered the split between the city, presented by Hegel as an organic and corporate whole, and the wilderness, presented by Schopenhauer as the preserve of the irrational will. American life-philosophy is a discourse, which is more or less conscious of its aims, on the relations between the separate self and the moral self. Whatever differences there may be among the American classical thinkers, they are all united on the supremacy of moral commitment over all other life-commitments: American life-philosophy provides a moral resolution for the existential problem of life-commitment. The following chapters will show how for each of the American classical philosophers an initial moment of doubting, whether transcendental, vital, or existential, is resolved into a worldview or over-belief that is aimed at promoting moral commitment to the affairs of the ongoing community. Included within each of the world pictures or visions is a critique of those attitudes toward life or forms of "spirit" that undermine and destroy moral community. The final chapter presents the view that these critiques of what may broadly be called "fanaticism" are the soundest elements of the American tradition of life-philosophy and are the core of what may be carried forward today in that tradition.

Neither Hegel nor Schopenhauer, the two most important transitional figures between the moral individualism of Kant and contemporary existential individuality, traveled to the frontiers of life or gazed into the abyss. The Hegelian phenomenology of spirit and Schopenhauer's scrutiny of the attitudes of the will drew near to the existential attitude but did not pull back the curtain of appearance. Except for William James, who in many instances advanced to positions that are parallel to those of Nietzsche, the American life-philosophers remained within the ambit defined by Hegel and Schopenhauer. Thus, again with the exception of James, they did not fully comprehend the difficulties involved in a moral response to the existential predicament of radical separation. The method of interpretation used in the following discussion acknowledges that, for the most part, American life-philosophy is pre-existentialist, and it understands American classical thought by judging it in the light of William James, its most advanced exponent. The work is divided into two broad segments in accordance with its interpretative key. The second and third chapters discuss American classical idealism, which achieves florescence in the thought of Josiah Royce and C. S. Peirce. In general, these two chapters defend the position that Royce and Peirce unify their world pictures with deeply religious visions: God is still alive for them. God dies in American life-philosophy with William James's experience of existential separation, and, with an account of that separation and its import for the analysis of life, the first part of the work is completed. The second half of the study, which begins at the midpoint of the fourth chapter, proceeds from James's postulation of a moral resolution for existential agony and then moves on, in the fifth and sixth chapters, to discuss the evasion of existential separation in the naturalistic life-philosophies of John Dewey and George Santayana. Dewey and Santayana are not treated in an altogether negative fashion, however, and their insights into human limitation and the structure of fanaticism are drawn out and clarified. Thus, the work is drawn toward the void glimpsed by James, is sucked into it, and then emerges out of it, as James did, with the assertion of the moral self. The seventh and final chapter presents some suggestions for how the moral self might be defended today.

The continuation of the tradition of American life-philosophy requires both an existential deepening of its foundations and a defense of its moral resolution for existential doubt and radical separation. The following discussion is an attempt to provide such depth and vindication, to help perpetuate the life of this philosophical tradition.

2

Josiah Royce

Among the group of American classical philosophers Josiah Royce presented the clearest and most complete statement of life-philosophy. In his *Lectures on Modern Idealism* Royce said that "a philosophy is inevitably an expression of a mental attitude which one assumes towards life and towards the universe."[1] In his earliest major work, *The Religious Aspect of Philosophy*, he distinguished between theoretic and religious types of philosophy. Theoretic philosophy "tries to find out what it can about the real world" and when "it makes this effort, it has to be perfectly indifferent to consequences." Religious philosophy, though it "dare not to be in opposition to the truths that theory may have established," seeks to know the value of these truths: "It seeks not merely the truth, but the inspiring truth."[2] The task of the religious philosopher is to search for "the ideal among the realities" and to judge those realities from the standpoint of the ideal. As Royce noted in *The World and the Individual,* one who loves philosophy is devoted to "seeking clearness of thought and a soul-stirring vision of the truth."[3]

Throughout his life as a thinker Royce consistently pursued the project of religious philosophy, attempting to express clearly and rationally an attitude toward life and toward the universe. His basic problem was posed for him in the initial distinction that he made between theoretic philosophy, which is regulated by the aim of clarity, and religious philosophy, which is guided by inspiration. He was pledged to abide by the truth, regardless of consequences, but he had also to be loyal to the quest for an inspiring truth, one that would stir the soul. Royce was squarely within the great tradition of Western philosophy. His problem was Plato's, that of reconciling being and goodness, of justifying rationally the proposition that being is good. Royce's life-philosophy grows out of his fundamental belief that human beings need to be reconciled satisfactorily to their lives and to the universe, and that the primary task of philosophy is to accomplish such a reconciliation through the instrument of speculative reason.

Royce's absolute idealism, the doctrine that reality is a set of purposive acts coordinated by a single perfect act, was so important to the pragmatic and naturalistic philosophers who broke with him, such as William James, John Dewey, and George Santayana, that they lost sight of his project and its existential depth. Royce's variation on the Western theme of reconciling being and goodness was framed by G. W. F. Hegel's uncompromising description of the apparent facts of human life. Hegel had noted in the introduction to his *Lectures on the Philosophy of History* that "a simple, truthful account of the miseries that have overwhelmed the noblest of nations and polities and the finest exemplars of private virtue forms a most fearful picture and excites emotions of the profoundest and most hopeless sadness, counter-balanced by no consoling result." According to Hegel, "in contemplating history as the slaughter-bench at which the happiness of peoples, the wisdom of states and the virtue of individuals have been sacrificed, a question necessarily arises: To what principle, to what final purpose, have these monstrous sacrifices been offered?"[4] Hegel's question is that of theodicy, the justification of God's ways to human beings. Posing this question presupposes, as Hegel understood, that such justification is needed and that it can be provided most adequately by philosophy. Royce accepted both of these presuppositions and followed Hegel's general path, departing from it only to personalize and make existential the longing for reconciliation.

Hegel's emphasis upon the problem of theodicy had a profound moral dimension. The attempt to show, by rational speculation, that the judgment that history is a slaughter-bench is not definitive, was primarily an effort to overcome a passive attitude toward life and toward the universe. Hegel noted that sorrow over the "universal taint of corruption," which is generated by the contemplation of historical fact, slides into "boredom." In order to escape from this boredom "we draw back into the vitality of the present, into our aims and interests of the moment; we retreat, in short, into the selfishness that stands on the quiet shore and thence enjoys in safety the distant spectacle of wreckage and confusion."[5] For Hegel a reflection that tries to ascend from particulars to general principles is doomed to end in "depressing emotions." The way of avoiding melancholy is to initiate reflection with rational principles.

The Hegelian insight into the needs of the self and the roots of its despair broods over the group of American classical philosophers and determines the construction of each one's life-philosophy. The problem of American life-philosophy is to provide reasons to overcome the boredom described by Hegel. Royce, whose solution was closest to that of Hegel, trusted in reason to provide an inspiring truth, whereas the American thinkers who challenged idealism turned to other faculties such as will and imagination. In each case, however, Hegel's critique of utilitarianism was made a presupposition. In Hegel's account of the need for theodicy, a selfish and calculating attitude toward life is the end result of a process that begins with the acknowledgment of apparent evil and passes through "the boredom with which sorrowful reflection threatens us." Hegel's "boredom" is one way of approaching the condition of radical separation, in which the self takes a passive and solipsistic view of its life and despairs of any reality beyond or behind the tissue of images presented to it. For Hegel this despair takes a moral form and is experienced as a loss of interest in participating in the public world, a lack of zest for self-transcendence. Fundamentally, Hegelian boredom is a lack of care or concern for life, the spiritual disease of *acedia*. Hegel believed that *acedia* was the result of being unable to think beyond the moment of consciousness in which the apparent evil in the world is acknowledged. Theodicy, which is thinking beyond apparent evil to the conclusion that being is good, provides a ground for overcoming the despair of boredom that does not involve the false separation of the self from the community that is imposed by utilitarianism.

The American classical philosophers followed Hegel in interpreting the condition of radical separation morally. Philosophy was for them, as it was for Hegel, an activity essential to the well-being of the community, a critical and rational mediation between self and other. The philosopher performed the social function of showing others how they might find a reason to live without succumbing to *acedia* and despair. Royce, who was a continuer of absolute idealism, exemplified the Hegelian project more clearly than the other American classical philosophers. Royce's vision of the philosopher was heroic and provides a measure against which all other such visions can be compared. In *The World and the Individual* he presents his most extensive development of the image of the philosopher as a lonely wanderer in the wilderness, an image that recurs frequently throughout his work. According to Royce, the "way of reflection is long" and the "forest of our common human ignorance is dark and tangled." He observes that people who are "content to live and to work only in regions where the practical labors of civilization have cleared the land" have drawn a happy lot. Philosophers do not choose happiness but are "by destiny" frontiersmen who must appear to others to be "mere" wanderers. The philosopher "knows best himself how far he wanders, and how often he seems to be discovering only new barrenness in the lonely wilderness." Philosophers, however, have an obligation to the community: "The frontiersman may wander; but he must some day win what shall belong to the united empire of human truth." The community is right to ask that "the student of philosophy shall find, if he succeeds at all, a living truth; and that the God of the wilderness, if indeed he be the true God, shall show himself also as the keeper of the city."[6]

The idea that the philosopher's task is to show that the wilderness and the city are ruled by the same God is a metaphorical way of saying that the philosopher's project is to reconcile being and goodness. The wilderness to which Royce refers is that of radical doubt about beliefs and conventions, while the city symbolizes the ongoing community sustained by those beliefs and conventions. The philosopher's gift to the community is a rational defense of the essence of its religious aspirations, a justification of faith by reason. In *The Religious Aspect of Philosophy* Royce described the "typical philosophic experience" as "first, then, the despair of a thorough-going doubt, and then the discovery that this doubt contains in its bosom the truth that we are sworn to discover, however we can." Royce's paradigm for philosophical activity is that by a withdrawal of the self into the despair of a thorough-going doubt (a retreat of the self into the wilderness), the beliefs that sustain the community gain rational security by reflection on the meaning of the doubt. Radical separation, which is essential to philosophy, is defended by Royce, but only on the condition that the separation be made for the benefit of all. The heroic philosopher, the philosopher as frontiersman, tames the wilderness of solipsistic thought by showing that it is not a wilderness at all, but the city seen from another angle. Thus, philosophy saves "our minds from hopeless, everlasting wandering," which is, for Royce, the most fearful condition. So much does Royce expect from philosophy that he declares in *The Religious Aspect of Philosophy* that "to resist the clarifying process, even while we undertake it, is to sin against what is best in us, and is also to sin against humanity."[7]

The images of "wilderness" and "city" are, perhaps, so vividly delineated by Royce because of all the American classical philosophers he was the only one who was brought up in the American West. Royce noted that the mining town in the Sierra Nevada, Grass Valley, California, in which he was born in 1855, had been founded only five years before his birth. As he grew up, however, he did not think of himself as living in a new land, but rather experienced "a very frequent wonder as to what my elders meant when they said that this was a new community." He "frequently looked at the vestiges left by the former diggings of miners, saw that many pine logs were rotten, and that a miner's grave was to be found in a lonely place not far from my own house." He wondered what there was "in this place that ought to be called new, or for that matter, crude" and "gradually came to feel that part of my life's business was to find out what all this wonder meant." Royce's wilderness, then, was from the beginning a mental and not a physical space, a place of wonder and doubt about received convictions, not of virgin land to be subdued. Indeed, his initial wonder was that the frontier should be considered a wilderness at all. It was in 1866, when he began to attend a large grammar school in San Francisco, that Royce—"redheaded, freckled, countrified, quaint, and unable to play boys' games"—was, through hazing by the other boys, introduced to the "majesty of the community."[8] His sense of separateness and difference, gained in the grammar-school experience, coupled with his early wondering and wandering, flow into his imagery of "wilderness" and "city." But behind that imagery is not the simple tale of a Californian who studied philosophy in Germany and taught at Harvard. It is, instead, the tale of a wondering child and a sensitive and insecure boy who both questioned the judgments of the community in the light of his personal experience and sought hungrily for full inclusion in the community.

As was argued in the preceding chapter, the condition of radical separation, when its structure is scrutinized deeply, does not of itself provide any exit from despair. Using Royce's imagery, the wilderness surrounds the city on all its sides and will always do so, however far the city pushes out. From the standpoint of radical separation there is no way of thinking oneself out of despair and any claim to have provided such a saving thought is grounded in an attenuation of existential despair into some more manageable or domesticated condition, usually a form of cognitive doubt. Any success, then, that Royce achieves in showing that the wilderness and the city are ruled by the same God, that being and goodness are in harmony, is based upon transforming the withering boredom that Hegel sought so desperately to avoid, into a predicament capable of intellectual resolution. In order to measure Royce's life-philosophy, it is necessary to sound the depth of his doubt.

Royce described the typical philosophical experience as a movement from "the despair of a thorough-going doubt" to the discovery that the doubt itself contains a truth that negates it. Royce's description of his own form of doubting appears in *The Religious Aspect of Philosophy* and is determinative over the rest of his thought. Having defined in his introductory chapter the primary problem of philosophy as the determination of "what it is that we ought to seek," Royce discusses his doubting in terms of uncertainty about "any fundamental principles upon which a sure knowledge of the world can be founded." Following in the Cartesian tradition he attempts to discover that of which he can be sure. He explores the question of whether there are "any certain judgments possible at all" and concludes: "From moment to moment one can be sure of each moment. All else is postulate."[9] This final resting place of doubt, "the present union of thought and sense," was called the "solipsism of the present moment" by George Santayana in *Scepticism and Animal Faith*. According to Santayana, that which appears in a present is the ultimate datum in the "order of evidence." However, Santayana noted that the datum of which we can be most certain is not necessarily indicative of the general structure of existence. In fact, for Santayana, whose break with idealism led him to a naturalistic philosophy, the appearances revealed in the present moment are late precipitates of a plastic matter and a primal will.

Royce's commitment was idealistic so he consistently did not seek an exit from the solipsism of the present moment by recourse to "animal faith" in a material world independent of conscious experience. Instead, Royce's "effort to accept nothing without criticism" led him to "a skepticism as nearly complete as is possible to any one with earnest activity of thought in him." Royce's skepticism, his brush with the despair of a thorough-going doubt, concerned the possibility of any true judgment beyond a report of the contents of the present moment. He had converted his original query about the ends that human beings ought to seek into a problem of theoretical truth. Royce escaped from his cognitive despair by arguing that if everything beyond the present is doubtful, then that doubt is only possible on the condition that there is at least one general truth, "namely, 'All but the immediate content of the present moment's judgment, being doubtful, we may be in error about it.' " From here Royce argues that the ground for the possibility of error is "an infinite unity of conscious thought to which is present all possible truth."[10] In summary, error is only possible in relation to truth and, because the standard of evidence is the appearance in a present moment, absolute truth must be the appearance in an eternal consciousness. Rather than leaping from the present moment to the postulation of a "realm of matter," as Santayana did, or linking the present moment to those adjoining it with "fringes," as William James did, Royce expanded the fleeting present of human consciousness into an eternal present held in an infinite span of attention by an absolute mind.

Royce's argument for absolute knowledge may be questioned at its inception. For the "one supposed general truth" that " 'All but the immediate content of the present moment's judgment, being doubtful, we may be in error about it' " may be substituted the assertion that "only the immediate content of the present moment's judgment is known with certainty." In the solipsism of the present moment it is not known with certainty that there is something beyond the present moment, so it is not known with certainty that it is appropriate to raise the possibility of error. If, as Royce argued, from moment to moment one can be sure of each moment and that all else is postulate, then doubt about the possibility of a true judgment beyond a report of the contents of the present moment is merely an aspect of the datum of a present moment. Royce seems to assume that the thought of a beyond vouchsafes the reality of that beyond, but, as Santayana argued, that assumption is unwarranted in a philosophy that claims to result "from the effort to accept nothing without criticism." Royce may be correct that we assume a beyond in our practical lives, that as finite beings our actions seek objects external to them, but he cannot guarantee a comprehensive reality by reflection upon the results of the transcendental method.

For the purposes of the present discussion, the questions just raised about the adequacy of Royce's argument for absolute knowledge are not decisive but are entered in order to indicate the logical basis upon which some of the other members of the group of American classical philosophers found Royce's reasoning to be deficient. As is often the case for philosophers, Royce's basic vision —the idea of an absolute knower modeled on the structure of a moment of conscious experience—was expressed in his first major work and elaborated upon throughout the rest of his career. As he reached the later phases of his reflections the vision became sharper and more intense, as works such as *The Philosophy of Loyalty* and *The Problem of Christianity* testify, and the attempt to demonstrate the necessity of the vision logically took on less importance. Royce's vision of the absolute was used by him to anchor "an expression of a mental attitude which one assumes towards life and towards the universe," what is called here a life-philosophy. The solipsism of the present moment, from which Royce derived his despair of a thoroughgoing doubt, is a pale reflection of the condition of radical separation, of Hegelian boredom. When it appears later in Santayana's mature reflections it will serve the same function of masking a deeper anguish and of preparing a cognitive bridge for reconciling human beings to their lives and to the cosmos.

The hallmark of Royce's voluntaristic idealism is the claim that just as judgments of truth and falsehood about fact imply an absolute totality of knowledge, so judgments about good and evil imply an absolute totality of goodness. According to Royce, human existence is essentially a quest for knowledge of its proper goal and for the means to that goal. In *The World and the Individual* Royce places each human action under a twofold limitation: "I neither know the whole of *what it is that I mean to do;* nor do I know more than the most insignificant fragment of *the facts that express my will.*"[11] Royce, then, makes doubt about purpose analogous to doubt about fact, arguing that the most fundamental human project is the gain of greater knowledge of the object of one's will and the means to it. For Royce, human beings are essentially wanderers whose deepest doubt is about their proper destination. Royce's thought is directed to demonstrating that what each one really means to do is what ought to be done. However, the limitations upon the knowledge of each finite being make it impossible for any individual to know in detail what should be done and how to do it. All that individuals can know with certainty, according to Royce, is that their lives have a purpose that is fulfilled in the eternal present of the absolute. Just because human beings doubt their purposes they can be in error about them, and because they can be in error about them they presuppose that they have true purposes. The argument for an idealistic life-philosophy in Royce's work is based upon the transformation of existential doubt into cognitive doubt and the resolution of cognitive doubt into cognitive certainty. For Royce, human beings are fundamentally knowers. They have the luxury of being primarily knowers because their lives have already been completed in the eternal will and thought. What remains their portion in existence is to learn more clearly what has been ordained for them.

The double limitation present in every human situation, that one knows neither one's purpose in detail nor the means to it, is not overcome and is not intended to be overcome in Royce's absolute idealism. Each individual still partakes of the wanderer's share with regard to the determination of finite acts, but, after philosophical reflection, with the assurance that, in principle, those acts are completed in a perfect harmony. As Royce noted in *The Religious Aspect of Philosophy*, the clarification of the mind is necessary "to save our minds from hopeless, everlasting wandering." Absolute idealism does not put an end to the wandering but insures that it is no longer hopeless and everlasting. Royce's idealistic life-philosophy is, in the sense of William James, an "overbelief." It does not provide and is not meant to provide concrete and practical guidance in the conduct of life, but is aimed at infusing life with a new inspiration. The philosopher, who wanders in the deserts and forests of doubt, returns to the city not with a blue-print for rebuilding it but with reasons for renewed commitment to its ongoing life. Hopeless and everlasting wandering through the tangles of skepticism removes the individual from participation in the public situation and fosters despair. Those who are content "to till the fertile fields and to walk in the established ways" should not be disturbed by the philosopher. Those who have been assailed by doubt need to be brought back to the community. From the journey into the wilderness the philosopher returns with a mediation for participation in the common life. The separated individual finds communion with others through the solidarity of all in the absolute. The wilderness and the city are, thus, revealed to have the same God.

In 1915, the year before his death, Royce observed in some remarks addressed to his friends at a banquet in his honor that after reviewing the entire "process" of his life he had concluded that "my deepest motives and problems have centred about the Idea of the Community, although this idea has only come gradually to my clear consciousness." Royce acknowledged that he had always been "a good deal of a nonconformist, and disposed to a certain rebellion," and that he had been "unpractical, —always socially ineffective as regards genuine 'team play,' ignorant of politics, an ineffective member of committees, and a poor helper of concrete social enterprises." He added that counterbalancing his "natural ineffectiveness in serving the community" was "the interest which has taught me what I nowadays try to express by teaching that we are saved through the community."[12] The preceding discussion has indicated that Royce's evaluation of his philosophical project was correct. Royce's first major work, *The Religious Aspect of Philosophy*, was published in 1885 when he was thirty years old and received his appointment as assistant professor of philosophy at Harvard. In this work he cast himself in the wanderer's role, withdrew to the despair of thoroughgoing doubt, and resolved his doubt through a philosophical act of deliverance to the absolute life. Fifteen years later, in his Gifford Lectures, published as *The World and the Individual*, Royce continued the imagery of the philosopher as the lonely wanderer in the wilderness of doubt and pledged himself to demonstrating that the same God ruled the wilderness and the city. In his later works, particularly *The Philosophy of Loyalty*, published in 1908, and *The Problem of Christianity*, published in 1913, the "Idea of the Community" as the reference for life-commitment was clearly expressed without very much recourse to the argumentation of technical idealism. Royce's last major work, *The Problem of Christianity*, is, in fact, more of a document of speculative theology than a work of technical philosophy. *The Problem of Christianity* closes the circle of Royce's life as a thinker, fulfilling the project of "religious philosophy" earlier announced in *The Religious Aspect of Philosophy*.

In *The Religious Aspect of Philosophy* Royce's final exit from solipsism of the present moment was not the argument to absolute knowledge from the determination of the grounds for the possibility of error, but the vision, which he believed the argument from error supported rationally, of "the *progressive realization by men of the eternal life of an Infinite Spirit.*" Resorting to the dialectic that structured all his reflections, Royce noted that from an ethical viewpoint human beings are obligated to devote themselves to art, science, the state, or "any like work" that tends to organize their lives "into one life." The ethical viewpoint is, in the terms of Royce's master imagery, the viewpoint of the city and is the first moment of the dialectic. The second moment of the dialectic is, of course, the withdrawal of the philosopher into the wilderness of doubt and the wresting of belief from the doubt. The third moment is the return to the city with a new justification for service to it which preserves both social bonds and individual judgment. For the "accidental expressions" of duty to specific pursuits Royce substitutes "one absolute expression": "*Devote yourselves to losing your lives in the divine life.* For all these special aims that we have mentioned are but means of accomplishing the knowledge of the fullness of the truth. And Truth is God."[13]

Devotion to the loss of one's life in a greater whole, however that whole be named, is the primordial design for life-commitment in American life-philosophy. The same design, as will be shown in succeeding chapters, governs the line of thought in classical American pragmatism that runs from C. S. Peirce through William James to John Dewey. Of the group of American classical philosophers only George Santayana, who expatriated himself, dissented from the demand for wholehearted deliverance. Royce's thought shows so clearly the dynamic of deliverance because its dialectic is based on an interpretation of the experience of philosophizing which, although it is presented in terms of universality, is an interpretation of what it means to philosophize in America. Even in *The Religious Aspect of Philosophy*, where he warns people to take heed lest their objects of worship be only their little pet infinities, Royce states that "no man has any business to set up his vocation as the highest one; and the man for whom truth is useful in his actual life-work as an inspiration, revealed to him only in feeling, is welcome to his feelings, is worthy of all regard from those whose vocation is philosophy, and shall not be tormented by our speculations."[14] The philosopher's vocation, then, is no greater than any other, and, because it demands the cultivation of doubt, carries dangers for the peace of the city. The first task of the philosopher in America is, therefore, to vindicate the right to philosophize. Although the Roycean philosopher is a hero, who bears the gift of an inspired truth, philosophical heroism is not likely to be widely acknowledged. Philosophers become suspect because they must radically separate themselves from the city and its "accidental" obligations. Once they have separated themselves their chief attention must be devoted to linking themselves to the community again, to showing that they are good citizens. The compulsion to rejoin the community is overwhelming for the American classical philosophers, so overwhelming that they raise deliverance to a universal obligation. In the background of their speculations is the nagging suspicion that their separation from the ongoing and concrete community was sinful or pathological. They make right their separation, justify it, by "teaching that we are saved through the community," as Royce said he did toward the end of his life. The community for which they speak, however, is not the actual and imperfect and limited one in which they live each day, but an ideal extension of it.

Royce's earliest statement of a directive for life-commitment was *"Devote yourselves to losing your lives in the divine life."* At the end of his philosophical career, in *The Problem of Christianity*, he reformulates that directive: "We are saved, if at all, by devotion to the Community. . . ." Royce derives the final statement of his life-commitment from a dialectical development of Arthur Schopenhauer's theory of the will. He begins by noting that the first attitude of the will (the first moment of the dialectic of the will) is the affirmation of the will to live, the form of which is the desire for self-assertion. Royce argues that the moment of affirmation is based upon "the natural solipsism of the individual will," which is benign so long as the individual will does not meet with opposition from other wills. But such opposition is inevitable and through its occurrence "primal solipsism" revives and mutual hatred ensues. Schopenhauer's escape from the war of all against all engendered by primordial self-assertion was resignation, the denial of the will to live, which is, for Royce, the second moment of the dialectic of the will. Royce does not believe that resignation, which he associates with mysticism, permits "the individual to win the true goal of life." He puts forward, in its place, a third attitude of the will, loyalty, which is "a positive devotion of the Self to its cause." As a dialectical synthesis of the first two attitudes of the will, loyalty sublates natural self-assertion by submitting it to a cause lying beyond the self but included within the absolute life. The cause, however, is not imposed upon the self but is acknowledged by the self to be its own. Royce associates the attitude of loyalty with Paul of Tarsus whose sacrifices for his cause "included the giving of whatever he possessed," but "never included the negation of the will, the plucking out of the root of all desire, in which Gotama Buddha found salvation: . . . Paul died at his conversion; but only in order that henceforth the life of the spirit should live in him and through him." Paul of Tarsus, then, is Royce's perfect exemplar of a devoted and delivered life. The essence of Pauline charity, according to Royce, is the "union of a longing for unity with a will which needs its own expression in works of loyal art."[15] The Christian life of Paul is a vital synthesis of affirmation of the will (a will that needs its own expression) and resignation (longing for unity) through "works of loyal art."

Royce's clearest defense of his overriding life-commitment appears at the conclusion of his dialectical development of the attitudes of the will. He remarks that for "a reasonable being" the "first practical principle, as well as the first theoretical presupposition," of philosophy "must" be: "Practically I cannot be saved alone; theoretically speaking, I cannot find or even define the truth in terms of my individual experience, without taking account of my relation to the community of those who know." From his first principle Royce infers that the community of knowers "is real whatever is real." Individuals who view themselves as if they were alone are not only doomed to failure but are "lost in folly." Royce concludes: "My life means nothing, either theoretically or practically, unless I am a member of a community."[16]

The community of which Royce speaks is proximately the actual society in which the individual lives but more fundamentally the world as a whole, the universal community which has God as its interpreter. The real will of each individual, the highest attitude of the will, "was the one which Paul knew as Charity, and as the life in and through the spirit of the Community."[17] For Royce, existence as charity was the fulfillment of the finite human will because it contained the practical acknowledgment, the enaction, of the theoretical truth that individuals cannot complete their meanings alone. In *The World and the Individual,* the systematic metaphysical work that stands between his early "religious philosophy" and his mature speculative theology, Royce argued that the mediation through which human beings connect their search for a final purpose or meaning for their lives to the absolute life is the ongoing social community. The absolute is not a god who is modeled on the finite individual, although greater in power and goodness, but a supreme life in which each being participates directly. God speaks to each self not through an inner call but through other selves: "*Our fellows furnish us the constantly needed supplement to our own fragmentary meanings.* That is, they help us to find out what our own true meaning is."[18]

Royce's life-philosophy, his commitment to deliver himself to the community, is grounded, then, on a fundamental will to meaning that overcomes both the natural tendency toward self-assertion and the denial of life engendered by the inevitable frustration of "primal solipsism." Salvation for Royce is the knowledge that one's deeds contribute to an ultimate purpose, that one's strivings to overcome *acedia* are not futile but intertwine with the efforts of others in the fabric of the absolute life. In the light of Royce's religious vision of existence it is puerile to criticize him, as William James did, for removing the sting from the struggle against evil. According to James, if reconciliation is an eternal accomplishment, then there is no ground for urging the strenuous life. Royce, whose spirit was deeply religious, commended the struggle against evil just because its success was guaranteed. His belief that being is good was the encouragement he needed to overcome Hegelian boredom. His spirit, which is that of the exemplary lives in Judaism, Christianity, and Islam, demands that each present moment be consecrated to God: "To view even the selfhood that passes away, even the deeds of the hour, as a service to God, and to

regard the life of our most fragmentary selfhood as the divine life
taking on human form, —this is of the deepest essence of religion."[19] The dedication of each moment to the service of God,
which Royce found at the heart of Pauline Christianity, is what
Dietrich Bonhoeffer called the life of "discipleship."[20] Royce
opened himself to James's critique by trying to demonstrate that
discipleship could be rationally justified and that its reward was
the completion of one's finite meanings. As Bonhoeffer revealed in
both his thought and his life, discipleship needs no external supports and, in fact, is corrupted by them. Royce's life-philosophy,
then, works its way to the limits of reason and passes over them
into vision and faith.

From the viewpoint of individuals seeking a mediation between
themselves and the absolute life, dedication to the community
forms the adequate bridge. From the deeper standpoint of philosophers seeking a mediation between themselves and the ongoing
community the proper bridge is the absolute life. The two perspectives show the ambiguous structure of the American philosophical experience. In Royce's version of that experience, the
idea of the absolute life is the philosopher's way of rejoining the
community after a sojourn in the wilderness of doubt. It is the philosopher's gift to the community that is meant to liberate human
beings from blind prejudice while binding them all the more
closely in solidarity. Dedication to the community is, for those
who have delivered themselves to the absolute life, the way of spe-
cifying their commitment, of making it concrete. In his metaphysical and theological speculations Royce took the viewpoint of the
wanderer searching for a way to return to the community without
compromising free and rational criticism. In his discussions of social ethics he took the standpoint of the individual seeking to serve
the absolute life concretely.

The late work, *The Philosophy of Loyalty*, published in 1908, contains Royce's most profound general discussion of social ethics.
Royce introduced his work, anticipating the "crisis philosophies"
of the twentieth century by more than a decade, with the observation that "one of the most familiar traits of our time is the tendency
to revise tradition, to reconsider the foundations of old beliefs, and
sometimes mercilessly to destroy what once seemed indispensable."[21] Royce had in mind particularly what he called Friedrich
Nietzsche's "transmutation of all moral values," which declared

the conventional morality of the past to be "a mere transition stage of evolution." Royce remarked that if "our moral standards are questioned, the iron of doubt—so some of us feel—seems to enter our very hearts." He proposed to overcome the doubt by a "deliberate centralization of all the duties and of all the virtues about the one conception of rational loyalty."

Royce develops the idea of loyalty in the same way as he discussed Pauline charity in *The Problem of Christianity*. Loyalty to a cause solves "the paradox of our ordinary existence" by uniting a cause transcendent to the self with a will internal to the self which delights in service, "and which is not thwarted but enriched and expressed in such service." Loyalty, then, is a synthesis of self-assertion and self-abnegation, just as charity is a synthesis of affirmation of the will to live and its denial. Royce, however, did not believe that the great problem of the contemporary era was the disloyalty of either selfishness or self-surrender, but loyalty to the wrong object given in the wrong spirit. The great social danger, according to Royce, was the "war-spirit" in which "power and service are at one," and the individual "has no will but that of the country." Royce foresaw the perversion of dedication to the community which would mark twentieth-century politics throughout the world and sought to provide a rational antidote for it. He understood that neither the individualist perfectionism of Nietzsche nor the socialist perfectionism of Marx would triumph over the demand of the self for significance and meaning. His analysis falls in the line of the Grand Inquisitor's dictum that "without a stable conception of the object of life, man would not consent to go on living, and would rather destroy himself than remain on earth, though he had bread in abundance."[22]

Royce's phenomenological description of loyalty as a sublation of the split in the unhappy consciousness between self-assertion and imposed demands provides his most powerful psychological insight into contemporary life. So long as human beings feel a tension between their own desires and the requirements of the social order in which they live they will be vulnerable to the idea that their only purpose is "to do the will of some fascinating social power." Here Royce sounds a theme that will recur in the writings of the other American classical philosophers. C. S. Peirce's critique of "party spirit," George Santayana's polemic against "fanaticism," and John Dewey's attack on "the quest for certainty" all place the focus of social ethics on a critique of the "war-spirit." This is the social and political side of the call of the American classical philosophers for devotion to the community and to the wider process of life. The city could not, after all, be trusted to go its own way. The philosopher's vocation, even if it was not higher than any of the others, was still essential to the community as a whole. The public function of the philosopher in America, which culminated in the career of John Dewey, was to be that of moral educator.

As a moral educator Royce taught that "if loyalty is the supreme good, the mutually destructive conflict of loyalties is in general a supreme evil." A "predatory cause," one that destroys the loyalties of others, is, therefore, an evil cause, "because it involves disloyalty to the very cause of loyalty itself." The ultimate principle of social morality, which functions in a like manner to Immanuel Kant's "categorical imperative," is, then, "loyalty to loyalty," which commands that one be "an aid and a furtherance of loyalty in my fellows." A social ethic that is given principle by loyalty to loyalty is Royce's antidote to the war-spirit and his means for realizing a solidary human community within the context of the "great community" of the absolute life. In concrete terms loyalty to loyalty is the basis of a liberal social order in which there is wide ideological tolerance and movement toward a social structure based on mutuality among various functional groups. However, Royce was not a utopian thinker and he acknowledged the possibility of conflicts of loyalties. The final judgment on what to do in any concrete situation rested with the individual guided by a rational conscience. The last word of such a conscience was: *"We are fallible, but we can be decisive and faithful; and this is loyalty."*[23] Here Royce looks forward to existentialism just as in his early work he looked backward to the attempted logical proofs of the absolute in classical idealism.

Royce's solution to the problem of *acedia*, which plagues modern thought and modern life, was commitment to a particular loyalty, regulated and leavened by the principle of loyalty to loyalty, and delivered to the absolute life in which all partial meanings are completed. The vital link in this solution is the middle term, loyalty to loyalty, which mediates between the particular and "accidental" object of primary loyalty and the over-belief in the absolute life. The mediating link, however, is the weakest one, because, as Royce admits, human beings are vulnerable to "vicious naïveté," the state in which they narrow their attention to their immediate concerns and lose sight of the general good, the maintenance of a social community in which each one's loyalty aids the loyalties of the others. Particular loyalties, rooted in the accidents of space and time, are vulnerable to the war-spirit. They are made to transcend that spirit only by deliverance to the absolute life. Without such dedication loyalty to loyalty is an abstract moral principle, incapable of inspiring the enthusiasm required for self-transcendence. Yet, as the previous discussion has shown, deliverance to the absolute life demands vision and faith, the commitment to discipleship. Royce's solution is religious in the strictest sense. It encourages the overcoming of Hegelian boredom, of the existential crisis of radical separation, by an inward conversion that then infuses life with a new spirit. Hegel's dictum that the normal course of *acedia* leads to escape from boredom into the narrow interests of the present moment is echoed by Royce in his warnings against the war-spirit. Both idealists attempt to counteract the blind deliverance to particularity, whether in its individualist or its collectivist forms, with remodeled versions of Christianity based on a social principle. Royce's version is more favorable to individual judgment than Hegel's is, but it is still a call to discipleship. Americans in the twentieth century did not heed that call. Royce, the heroic philosopher, guilty for his separation, did not convince them that the wilderness and the city were ruled by the same God.

3

C. S. Peirce

In his preface to *The Problem of Christianity* Josiah Royce attempted to free himself from the mantle of "the common tradition of recent idealism" and stated that as to certain metaphysical doctrines, "I now owe much more to our great and unduly neglected American logician, Mr. Charles Peirce, . . . than I ever have owed, at any point of my own philosophical development, to the doctrines, which with technical accuracy, can be justly attributed to Hegel."[1] Royce was, in this passage, referring to his own "doctrine of signs," the thesis that "the universe consists of real Signs and of their interpretation," which he derived from Peirce's idea that "interpretations have, as the objects which they interpret, Signs." Royce's acknowledgment of Peirce was reciprocated by the latter in a brief introduction that he drafted to "The Fixation of Belief" around 1903. Peirce remarked there that he "continues to acknowledge, not indeed the Existence, but yet the Reality, of the Absolute, nearly as it has been set forth, for example, by Royce in his *The World and the Individual,* a work not free from faults of logic, yet valid in the main."[2] Royce's statement of his debt to Peirce and Peirce's affirmation of the idea of the absolute show a continuity within the thought of American classical philosophy which is obscured by labels such as "idealism," "pragmatism," and "naturalism." Such labels are necessary to anchor and situate a body of thought, but they should not be understood to indicate abysses separating philosophers who shared a common intellectual environment and common problems and concerns.

Charles Sanders Peirce was the oldest of the American classical philosophers, born sixteen years before Royce, in 1839. In the present discussion Peirce and the other American classical philosophers are interpreted against the background of Royce because Royce's attempt to systematize life-philosophy brought out sharply themes that are sometimes only partially developed in the other thinkers. Peirce, in particular, rebelled against the spirit of system and, rather than defining his thought, characterized it by a variety of names, some of which appeared to be in contradiction with one another, such as "prope-positivism," "Scholastic realism," "pragmaticism," and "Schelling-fashioned idealism," among many others. He described his philosophy as "the attempt of a physicist to make such conjecture as to the constitution of the universe as the methods of science may permit, with the aid of all that has been done by previous philosophers."[3] Emphasis should be placed here on the conjectural character of Peirce's thought. He put forward many theses and doctrines, some of which he held constantly throughout his work, but he held them hypothetically. The deepest core of Peirce's thought is "fallibilism," the principle that human judgments should be open to correction. Fallibilism is Peirce's absolute and is the ground of the life-commitments that he urges.

Peirce's thought is deeply moral, providing an ethical mediation between science and religion. As a "physicist," making "such conjecture as to the constitution of the universe as the methods of science may permit," he taught that the essence of science is its "spirit." Critiquing the "dictionary definition" of science as "systematized knowledge," Peirce argued that "we might even say that knowledge is not necessary to science," but that science is constituted by "correct method." However, even the method of science is a "scientific result" that was historically achieved, so that this method should not be regarded "as essential to the beginnings of science." That which is essential to science is, for Peirce, "the scientific spirit, which is determined not to rest satisfied with existing opinions, but to press on to the real truth of nature."[4] Peirce's philosophy is, most generally, an analysis and defense of the scientific spirit, not only as a guide to the conduct of inquiry but as a way of living in the most comprehensive sense. Peirce was enabled to generalize the scientific spirit to the foundation of life-philosophy because he identified that spirit with the essence of religion. In his earliest philosophical writing, an address delivered when he was twenty-four years old, Peirce argued that "from the moment when the ball of human progress received its first impetus from the mighty hands of Descartes, of Bacon, and of Galileo, we hear, as the very sound of the stroke, the decisive protest against any authority, however venerable, against any arbiter of truth except our own reason." According to Peirce the submission to reason is the hallmark of modern civilization and "civilization is nothing but Christianity on the grand scale." Christians, he claimed, "must believe that Christ is now directing the course of history and presiding over the destinies of kings, and that there is no branch of the public weal which does not come within the bounds of his realm." Just as in Royce's religious thought, the theme of discipleship centers Peirce's interpretation of Christianity: " 'His service is perfect freedom.' We are accustomed to say that [this phrase is] hyperbolical. But that is an unwarrantable assumption —a mere subterfuge to reconcile the statement with the fact."[5]

As Peirce's thought matured he put greater emphasis on the submission of reason to experience, but he maintained his religious commitment, particularly to the unity of science and religion, and to the life guided by discipleship. In his address of 1863 he projected a spiritual vision of history which leavened and informed his later thought. Peirce divided history into three stages, the first of which was "the egotistical age when man arbitrarily imagined perfection." The present era, he thought, was an "idistical stage" in which observation of perfection has replaced imagination of it. The final historical stage would be a "tuistical" one in which human beings shall be "in communion" with perfection.[6] In the final stage, according to Peirce, human beings will see the "folly" of saying that nature was created for their use. Poetry, associated with the egotistical stage, "shall be no more"; even "the progress of science may die away." Human beings will see "God's wisdom and mercy, not only in every event of" their own lives, "but in that of the gorilla, the lion, the fish, the polyp, the tree, the crystal, the grain of dust, the atom." The vision of the tuistical era will be aesthetic, but its beauty will have been purified of the arbitrary fantasies of the egotistical age by the skepticism and materialism of the present idistical era. Here Peirce's early thought bears Hegelian tracings, being structured by a dialectic in which the first moment is unselfconscious and subjective unity, the second is a conscious disunity of subject and object, and the third is self-conscious unity of subject and object in a clarified totality. Peirce's vision of the tuistical era, formed by communion of self and world, structured his later thought, keeping it close to the texture of lived experience and driving it away from abstract systematization. The idea of communion is one of the experiences of concrete perfection, of immediate appreciation of life, purified of its discontinuities and frustrations. As against such an ideal of plenitude, which Peirce associated with the great religions, particularly with Christianity, logical unifications of the cosmos seemed to be pale and false to life's exuberance and spontaneity.

Peirce's early dialectic is in one respect an inversion of Auguste Comte's three stages of history—the theological, the metaphysical, and the positive. Indeed, Peirce and Comte agree about the first stage, in which human wishes govern the interpretation of events in the world. However, Peirce's second stage, the idistical, collapses Comte's metaphysical and positive eras into one. The tuistical stage is, of course, where Peirce breaks radically with Comte by restoring comprehensive vision and valuing humility and appreciation over prediction and control. In his idea that in the final stage of history human beings will see the folly of saying that nature was created for their use, Peirce anticipates the critics of humanism, such as Martin Heidegger, who argue that the crisis of contemporary civilization centers on the overwhelming tendency to repose dignity in human being, particularly in species being, rather than in being itself.

Throughout his life as a thinker Peirce consistently challenged positivism, bringing forward the vision of communion that he first expressed in the address of 1863. In a symposium published in 1887, for example, Peirce challenged the mechanistic interpretation of scientific law advanced by Herbert Spencer by appealing to the direct and lived experience of nature: "When we gaze upon the multifariousness of nature we are looking straight into the face of a living spontaneity. A day's ramble in the country ought to bring that home to us."[7] Peirce's tuistical vision reached its culmination in his mature thought in the idea of "evolutionary love," which was contained in papers published in the *Monist* in the early 1890s. Anticipating Sigmund Freud's discussion of the life instincts, Peirce remarks that at its inception "philosophy, when just escaping from its golden pupa-skin, mythology, proclaimed the great evolutionary agency of the universe to be Love." He calls this love "Eros, the exuberance-love," which may be understood to be the principle lending integrity to living spontaneity. Peirce compares his hypothesis that the cosmos is structured by a tendency toward the spontaneous harmony of living processes ("agapastic evolution") with the Darwinian idea that evolution proceeds by chance variations ("tychasm") and the Hegelian supposition that evolution is determined by a rigid developmental law prescribing abrupt leaps between successive stages ("anancasm"). Peirce discusses the idea of evolutionary love mainly in relation to the history of human thought, noting that "the agapastic development of thought is the adoption of certain mental tendencies, not altogether heedlessly, as in tychasm, nor quite blindly by the mere force of circumstances or of logic, as in anancasm, but by an immediate attraction for the idea itself, whose nature is divined before the mind possesses it, by the power of sympathy, that is by virtue of the continuity of mind."[8]

There is a deep relation between Peirce's early and his mature thought on the cosmos. Tychastic evolution is analogous to the egotistical stage of thought, in that both are marked by arbitrary assertion; anancastic evolution is the counterpart of the idistical stage of mental development, in that both alienate free consciousness from external determination; and agapastic evolution corresponds to the tuistical era of thinking, in that both are based on a process of sympathetic communion among beings. The ground of communion, of agapastic evolution, which Peirce sought in his mature thought, is direct comprehension of transindividual mental continuity: "The agapastic development of thought should, if it exists, be distinguished by its purposive character, this purpose being the development of an idea. We should have a direct agapic or sympathetic comprehension and recognition of it, by virtue of the continuity of thought."[9] Direct comprehension of mental continuity is achieved, Peirce believed, for the individual in the experience of the continuity of feeling: "There is no doubt about one idea affecting another, when we can directly perceive the one gradually modified and shaping itself into the other."[10] Peirce also believed that transindividual mental continuity is indirectly supported by "the purposive character of many great movements" and by the fact that great ideas, particularly in the sciences, have occurred "simultaneously and independently to a number of individuals of no extraordinary general powers." But he confessed himself unable to "produce a cogent demonstration" that "there is such an entity as the 'spirit of an age' or of a people, and that mere individual intelligence will not account for all the phenomena."[11] Even in Peirce's mature thought communion remained primarily a vision, though one that was backed, he thought, by good reasons.

Peirce's concern for the reconciliation of the egotistical and the idistical stages of human development is paralleled in the thought of the other American classical philosophers. Royce, for example, in *The World and the Individual*, contrasted "the world of description," the set of ontological presuppositions assumed by natural science, with "the world of appreciation," the set of presuppositions guiding a community of moral individuals. According to Royce, prior to civilization all nature had been mythologically endowed with consciousness and the rudiments of personality. In the present civilized era, however, nature as interpreted by science had been divested of final causes, whereas society had progressively acknowledged the freedom and intrinsic value of its members. Royce believed that his absolute idealism would heal the rift between "physical reality" and "social reality" by reanimating the cosmos on a rational basis.

The dialectic that Peirce presented in his earliest reflections and that shaped his later thought, and Royce's dialectic of the worlds of description and appreciation show that Hegel's philosophy had a profound and lasting effect upon American life-philosophy, despite Royce's protestations that he owed relatively little to Hegel's inspiration. In both Peirce's and Royce's works, as well as in the writings of George Santayana and John Dewey, the dialectic is used to critique the separation of human beings from nature and, therefore, is an antidote to the *hybris* attending industrialization. In fact, American classical philosophy is better interpreted as a corrective to the spirit of manipulation and control than as a defense of that spirit. Royce was concerned that in the modern age human beings had lost their solidarity with the rest of nature, that they were treating nature as a series of means, rather than as the divine body. Santayana, in *Three Philosophical Poets*, sought union with nature through the great works of "philosophical poetry," such as Lucretius's *On the Nature of Things*, Dante's *Divine*

Comedy, and Goethe's *Faust,* which he believed tempered the pretensions of imagination with acceptance of human limitation. In Santayana's dialectic, an initial stage in which wish is projected on the world is succeeded by a separation of wish from fact, which in turn is made beautiful by philosophical poetry. John Dewey, who was the most sophisticated dialectician among the American classical philosophers, persistently urged that the industrial means of transforming nature be brought under ethical control. In *The Quest for Certainty* he adumbrates a doctrine of "purposive evolution," in which human beings, who are the highest expressions of nature, commit themselves to the task of being stewards of nature. The American classical philosophers differ from their counterparts in Europe, not because they are apostles of scientific technology and progressivism (which, in the main, they are not), but because they try to find a place for science in a wider spiritual economy.

Within the general project of American classical philosophy of finding a reconciliation between human beings and nature, Peirce's contribution is the most vitalistic, the closest to a prayer to life. Peirce was, perhaps, enabled to affirm a thoroughgoing fallibilism with regard to cognitive judgments because he had a more immediate trust in the underlying life-process. His challenge to positivism on the basis of a look "straight into the face of a living spontaneity" indicates his native trust, as do some of his manuscript notes toward a critique of positivism: "All men and all animals love life. . . . The *love of life* is more than the love of sensuous life: it is also a love of rational life."[12] The encompassing love of life expressed here by Peirce undergirds his stringent analyses of the logic of science. He has a direct appreciation of the irreducibility of the "qualities of feeling," which he gathered under his category of "firstness" and which kept him from substituting general ideas for lived experiences. He was not tempted by system, perhaps, because he was in closer communion with life than Royce was. Resonances of *acedia* are faint in Peirce's writings whereas they color nearly all Royce's thought.

The deepest breach between the philosophies of Royce and Peirce appears in their respective discussions of doubt. In his address of 1863 Peirce asserted that Descartes, Bacon, and Galileo had all given the modern spirit its impetus through their rebellion "against any arbiter of truth except our own reason." Indeed,

Peirce praised Descartes as "the father of modern metaphysics," who "introduced the term 'philosophic doubt'" and who declared "that a man should begin every investigation entirely without doubt; and he followed a completely independent train of thought, as though, before him, nobody had ever thought anything correctly."[13] Royce, as was noted in the preceding chapter, continued in the Cartesian tradition by attempting a comprehensive doubt, which he recorded in *The Religious Aspect of Philosophy* and which resulted in the solipsism of the present moment. He did not abandon this starting point throughout his career as a thinker and modeled his absolutism on the human experience of a present moment. Peirce, in contrast, made a decisive break with the Cartesian spirit, basing his mature reflections on a new interpretation of doubt.

Peirce's challenge to Cartesian doubt is first developed in his 1868 article "Some Consequences of Four Incapacities" and then perfected in his 1877 article "The Fixation of Belief." He begins the first essay by stating again that Descartes is "the father of modern philosophy" and that the first characteristic of the "spirit of Cartesianism" is "that philosophy must begin with universal doubt," whereas the previous scholasticism "had never questioned fundamentals." Peirce responds to the Cartesian spirit by asserting that "we cannot begin with complete doubt." Rather, philosophers "must begin with all the prejudices that they initially have, because these prejudices are things that it does not occur to them can be questioned." Initial skepticism about what is actually believed "will be a mere self-deception, and not real doubt." Peirce concludes his discussion with the injunction: "Let us not pretend to doubt in philosophy what we do not doubt in our hearts."[14]

Peirce renews his critique of Cartesian doubt in "The Fixation of Belief" where he defends his "proposition" that "the settlement of opinion is the sole end of inquiry" against the idea that inquiry should begin with questioning everything. He proposes that "there must be a real and living doubt, and without this all discussion is idle." In a note added to the manuscript in 1893 Peirce elaborates, arguing that "where no real doubt exists in our minds inquiry will be an idle farce, a mere whitewashing commission which were better let alone."[15] Peirce's critique of Cartesian doubt is both logical and moral. Logically, he claims that it is impossible actually to doubt what one does not doubt: feigned doubt is self-contradictory. Morally, he condemns feigned doubt as "an idle farce." There is no problem in understanding Peirce's moral point. Philosophers, according to him, should not invent problems that are unrelated to those that arise in the conduct of other human activities. Lived doubt, for Peirce, is an irritated state of mind that causes a struggle to attain a state of belief. He is unsympathetic to gratuitous irritation, because it diverts attention from more real problems and, perhaps more important, because it is in bad faith; it is a pretense to irritation. Peirce's logical point, however, is less intelligible. Surely he is correct that it is not possible to doubt what one does not doubt. But the force of that statement depends upon how doubt is defined. If Peirce means only to say that he defines doubt as "real and living doubt," and that what Descartes undertook was not doubt at all but something else, then he is on secure logical grounds. But if he means that the Cartesian method is logically self-contradictory he is on shakier ground, because how can he then turn around and declare it to be an idle farce "better let alone"? Either feigned or methodical doubt is a determinate mental activity that, according to Peirce, should not be undertaken, or it is not an activity at all, but an illusion, and any injunctions against it are misplaced. In general, Peirce's thought supports the interpretation of Cartesian doubt as a determinate mental activity that he holds should not be undertaken for moral reasons, primarily because it alienates from direct contact with concrete life and from the philosopher's solidarity with others. But Peirce's effort here to buttress morality with "logic" is paralleled elsewhere in his work and recalls Royce's efforts to reason his way to the absolute.

Peirce's defense of "real and living doubt" is tied to the idea, which is expressed often in his manuscripts, that experience is constituted by "the compulsion, the absolute constraint upon us to think otherwise than we have been thinking."[16] Peirce's trust in lived experience extends to his principle that doubt arises only within a context of stable habits and that, therefore, the destiny of doubt is to be resolved into new habits. When human beings encounter circumstances for which their stock of habits is inadequate they suffer the irritation of doubt, the difference between reality and fantasy forces itself upon them, and they search for more appropriate patterns of conduct. The struggle to attain a state of belief and, thus, to dispel the irritation of doubt is Peirce's definition of inquiry. The task of the logician, according to Peirce, is to evaluate the methods of inquiry, the ways in which belief may be fixed. It is with regard to the fixation of belief that Peirce's objections to the Cartesian method of doubting are brought out most clearly. The Cartesian method is a quest for certainty that "teaches that the ultimate test of certainty is to be found in the individual consciousness." Peirce argues, in opposition to the doctrine that single individuals are "absolute judges of truth," that "we individually cannot reasonably hope to attain the ultimate philosophy which we pursue; we can only seek it, therefore, for the *community* of philosophers."[17] Cartesian doubt is not only immoral because it is idle, but because it draws its practitioners away from the community of inquirers, the task of which is to resolve the real and living doubts that arise in the course of everyday life.

The most serious gap in Peirce's life-philosophy is his failure to provide any reasons why philosophers have undertaken comprehensive doubting in the modern era. He notes that "scholasticism had rested on the testimony of sages and of the Catholic Church" and that science rests on the agreement of a scientific community that is regulated by certain logical methods, themselves open to revision. However, he does not account for the emergence in modern times of the individual consciousness as the seat of philosophical judgment. Why have thinkers engaged in the "idle farce" of holding what they actually believe open to a feigned doubt? It is no small matter that Peirce does not address this question, because his break with the modern tradition is made on the issue of doubt. He reaches back across nearly three hundred years of speculative thought, which was based upon the Cartesian method, to make contact with scholastic philosophy. His new life-philosophy, which replaces the Church with an idealized scientific community, emphasizes shared commitment to methods and to the spirit of dissatisfaction with existing opinions, rather than an allegiance to broad substantive beliefs. As was noted in the first chapter, the essence of modern philosophy is the radical separation of the self from involvement in that which is other than itself. Descartes's method of systematic doubting is, in the context of radical separation, a cognitive substitution for a deeper existential predicament. Royce, in his retreat to solipsism of the present moment, brushed against the more radical existential doubt, which Unamuno called "agonic," but fled from it into a skepticism about the possibility of objective truth. Peirce does not deepen the Cartesian method and provide it with an existential dimension, but shifts the locus of doubt to everyday troubles. A "real and living doubt" is that which can, in principle, be resolved by cooperative inquiry.

The import of Peirce's break with Cartesianism becomes clear in his most extended discussion of life-commitment, which appears in the article, "The Doctrine of Chances," published in 1878. Within the context of clarifying the logic of probabilistic inference Peirce introduces the thesis that social sentiment is presupposed in reasoning. He begins his analysis by describing a hypothetical situation in which a person is presented with two packs of cards, one of which contains twenty-five reds and one black, and the other, twenty-five blacks and one red. If a red card is chosen the individual will be transported to "eternal felicity," but if a black one is drawn the individual will experience "everlasting woe." Peirce argues that it would be "folly to deny" that the person ought to prefer the pack containing more reds, though there is no second chance. However, if the black card is drawn from the red deck, the individual would have no consolation: "He might say that he had acted in accordance with reason, but that would only show that his reason was absolutely worthless." Peirce concludes that "there can be no sense in reasoning in an isolated case at all."[18]

As the next step in his argument Peirce claims that the predicament of an individual leading a life is not different in kind from that of the person drawing a card to determine ultimate destiny. The "number of risks, the number of probable inferences, which a man draws in his whole life is a finite one, and he cannot be absolutely *certain* that the mean result will accord with the probabilities at all." Death, according to Peirce, "makes the number of our risks, of our inferences, finite, and so makes their mean result uncertain." Yet the "very idea of probability and of reasoning rests on the assumption that this number is indefinitely great." Peirce, then, has led up to the point that it is not possible for individuals, considered merely as finite beings, to lead their lives in accordance with logic. He sees "but one solution" to the problem of reconciling logic and life, and that is for individuals not to limit their interests. Interests "must not stop at our own fate, but must embrace the whole community." And Peirce's community, like Royce's, is not finite, but extends "to all races of beings with whom we can come into immediate or mediate intellectual relation," and even "beyond this geological epoch, beyond all bounds." Peirce concludes his argument with the declaration: "He who would not sacrifice his own soul to save the whole world is, as it seems to me, illogical in all his inferences, collectively. Logic is rooted in the social principle."[19]

Just as Royce did, Peirce identifies his call for deliverance to community with Pauline Christianity. He draws from his "logical" argument for deliverance three "logical sentiments" which he makes analogous to St. Paul's triad of charity, faith, and hope. Returning to the case of the individual choosing to draw a card from one of two decks, he remarks that "he cannot be logical so long as he is concerned only with his own fate, but that that man who should care equally for what was to happen to all possible cases of the sort could act logically, and would draw from the pack with the most red cards." Thus, Peirce's analogue to charity is "conceived identification of one's interests with those of an unlimited community." The analogue to faith is recognition of the possibility of the interest in the unlimited community being made supreme and Peirce's hope is in "the unlimited continuance of intellectual activity." He states that his three "logical sentiments" are "indispensable requirements of logic." Peirce admits that there can be no reasons for thinking that any "intellectual race," including humanity, will exist forever, but he adds that "there can be no reason against it." Anticipating William James's "will to believe," Peirce states that "as the whole requirement is that we should have certain sentiments, there is nothing in the facts to forbid our having a *hope*, or calm and cheerful wish, that the community may last beyond any assignable date."[20]

It is difficult to assess the force of Peirce's argument for surrender of one's own interests to the interest of a hypothetical unlimited community. In "The Fixation of Belief" Peirce defines human beings as imperfect logical animals and says that "logicality in regard to practical matters" is "the most useful quality an animal can possess."[21] However, even if Peirce is correct that in order to decide "logically" it is necessary to identify one's interests with those of an unlimited community, the choice to be logical in this respect is not a "practical matter." Rather, he would have it be a pledge of one's whole being to an absolute commitment. The identification of one's interests with those of an unlimited community is not subject to revision, is not a hypothesis, but is a deliverance of one's life. But what is the ground of a commitment to be "logical" in Peirce's sense? Peirce's argument seems to follow a Kantian line, moving toward the same sort of appeal to consistency that marks the defense of lived doubt against Cartesian doubt. Under this interpretation Peirce's point would be that whenever we make prudential judgments, if we scrutinize those judgments sufficiently, we are identifying our specific decisions with an unlimited number of like decisions. Our specific decisions are justified logically only if we treat them as instances in a series. The logic of prudential judgment is such that in order to justify a self-interested act it is necessary to appeal to an unlimited series of such acts. Hence, the individual who draws from the red deck because of an equal concern for what would happen in all cases acts logically, whereas one who does the same thing for selfish motives acts illogically. The primary difference between Kant's argument in *The Foundations of the Metaphysics of Morals* and Peirce's is that Peirce's imperative seems to be to act prudently, whereas Kant's is to act in accordance with a universal law of reason, which is sometimes imprudent from the individual's viewpoint. If the suggested interpretation be accepted, however, there is no ground for claiming that "he who would not sacrifice his own soul to save the whole world is . . . illogical." The "unlimited community" to which prudential judgments are referred is ideal, not existent. It is not an object of loyalty, but is, like Kant's "kingdom of ends," an abstraction. It cannot be the ground of self-sacrifice, but only of self-interest.

Peirce's argument does not succeed in grounding "the social principle" logically. As he even accedes in his discussion of the three logical sentiments, his hope that the present "intellectual race," humanity, will persist indefinitely is not rationally justified. The deeper ground of Peirce's call for deliverance to the community is, of course, a religious vision that develops out of his early concern for communion, his promise of a "tuistical" stage of human development, and his idea of evolutionary love. One of the most complete expressions of this vision is found in some notes that Peirce attached in 1893 to his article, "How to Make Our Ideas Clear." Providing interpretation of the pragmatic maxim, that our conceptions of the effects, that might conceivably have practical bearings, of the object of our conception is the whole of our conception of that object, Peirce states that the maxim should not be understood in "too individualistic a sense." Enunciating a view of history with marked Hegelian tracings, Peirce interprets "effects" in a radically collectivist sense: "To say that man accomplishes nothing but that to which his endeavors are directed would be a cruel condemnation of the great bulk of mankind, who never have leisure to labor for anything but the necessities of life for themselves and their families. But, without directly striving for it, far less comprehending it, they perform all that civilization requires, and bring forth another generation to advance history another step. Their fruit is, therefore, collective; it is the achievement of the whole people." Peirce grounds his interpretation of history ontologically, claiming that study of "the great principle of continuity" shows that "all is fluid and every point directly partakes the being of every other." His initial claim that the fruits of human activity are collective deepens and is transformed into the theses that "individualism and falsity are one and the same," and that "man is not whole as long as he is single, that he is essentially a possible member of society." Peirce observes that each one's experience is "nothing" if it stands alone, noting that if an individual sees what others do not "we call it a hallucination: . . . It is not 'my' experience, but 'our' experience that has to be thought of; and this 'us' has indefinite possibilities."[22] Peirce concludes his note by claiming that individual action is a means, not an end, and that individual pleasure is also not our end; "we are all putting our shoulders to the wheel for an end that none of us can catch more than a glimpse at—that which the generations are working out." According to Peirce, who follows here in the idealist tradition, that end will consist in "the development of embodied ideas."

Peirce's vision of the solidarity of all being and of the special historical solidarity of human beings is reminiscent of the expressions of mysticism that appear throughout Dostoevsky's writings, especially in the mystical experiences of Father Zossima in *The Brothers Karamazov*. Zossima, for example, remarks that "everywhere in these days men have ceased to understand that the true security is to be found in social solidarity rather than in isolated individual effort." He counterposes isolated individualism to his mystical vision that "all is like an ocean, all is flowing and blending; a touch in one place sets up movement at the other end of the earth."[23] Thus Dostoevsky's vision of human existence, like Peirce's, is structured by a polarity between rebellious individualism and an underlying continuity of life. Such figures as Raskolnikov, Ivan Karamazov, and the underground man exemplify the separation of the individual from society, a separation that is undertaken in resentment against finitude and limitation, and that involves an absolute declaration of freedom from moral law, the "freedom to be free." In Dostoevsky's world the criminal is the paradigm for the rebellious individual and overcoming rebellion demands confession, repentance, and inner acceptance of the justice of punishment. The individual must, according to Dostoevsky, intuit the unity of being in order to constitute a proper relation to life; reasoning is not sufficient to secure a correct orientation of existence. The respect in which Dostoevsky's view differs from that of Peirce is in Dostoevsky's insistence upon the reality of freedom of the will. Individualism, for Dostoevsky, is false, but it is not illusory, a thesis that indicates an opacity in human being, a fundamental mystery. For Peirce, there seems to be no such mystery. He expresses a vision of communion, of what he calls in some of his later writings "synechism," but he does not counterpose this vision to the fact of self-assertion, which was apparent, for example, to Royce. Peirce is satisfied to argue that in some sense individualism is illogical and that "those who dwell continually upon their expectations are apt to become oblivious to the requirements of their actual situation."[24] Peirce's basic trust in lived experience, which is rooted in mystical vision, results in his doctrine that the individual is an illusory entity. His logical attacks on individualism float on the surface of this deeper visionary current and draw their impetus from it. The attacks, however, invariably fall short of their mark because they do not concede the reality of their object, the individual will.

As was noted above, whereas the spiritual state of *acedia* plays a prominent role in Royce's reflections on religion, it is scarcely discernible as an element in Peirce's speculations. One of the reasons for the absence of concern for *acedia* in Peirce's thought, it was suggested, is the closeness of his informing vision to lived experience. Yet *acedia* is as much an experience as any other and was particularly available to thinkers who philosophized against the background of Hegel. Peirce, one might surmise, was sensitive enough to have experienced *acedia* and to have grappled with it existentially. One tell-tale hint of a brush with "world sickness" appears in "How to Make Our Ideas Clear" where Peirce remarks that "many a man has cherished for years as his hobby some vague shadow of an idea, too meaningless to be positively false; he has, nevertheless, passionately loved it, has made it his companion by day and by night, and has given to it his strength and his life . . . , and then he has waked up some bright morning to find it gone, clean vanished away like the beautiful Melusina of the fable, and the essence of his life gone with it." And then Peirce cryptically adds: "I have myself known such a man. . . ." That Peirce was himself the man to whom the remarks referred is suggested by the fact that his first wife was named Harriet Melusina Fay. Peirce's polemic against feigned doubt is balanced throughout his work by the insistence that the scientific spirit is dissatisfaction with existing opinions. While the normal process of human life is to be content with existing habits, as long as they do not provoke irritation, "feigned hesitancy, whether feigned for amusement or with a lofty purpose, plays a great part in the production of scientific inquiry."[25] Peirce, in fact, writes of "merely fancying myself to be in a state of hesitancy because I am bored with having nothing to trouble me." If, indeed, Peirce's remarks indicate that he had experienced *acedia*, then he, like Royce, may have escaped from radical separation and have made his connection to the ongoing community by teaching others how to be moral.

Both Peirce and Royce teach deliverance of the self to the community, attempting to ground their injunctions in rational argumentation, but actually basing them more deeply on religious vision and the call to discipleship. In the cases of Peirce and Royce, the community to which the individual is delivered is not a finite and temporal unity but an ideal entity embracing, ultimately, the entire living cosmos. The individual's judgment is preserved, there is no submission to a finite or worldly authority, but there is obedience to an inner calling amplified by concrete religious experience of solidarity and continuity with the world as a whole. Neither Peirce nor Royce gives explicit and specific moral directives. Their ethical thought is in the service of an over-belief that, in the terms of Paul Tillich, "centers" life. In working their ways to their life-commitments Peirce and Royce confront comprehensive doubt and find escapes from it, not by deepening it to agonized doubt, but by forging links between being and goodness. They find their ways out of or around radical separation by a fusion of religion and morality in a commitment to the ongoing community. Their commitment, of course, is special: to teach commitment to the community to its members. But for them the teaching of morality is a religio-moral vocation.

Just as it was for Royce, the greatest danger to the moral life that Peirce identifies is narrow or parochial commitment to society. In his article, "Evolutionary Love," published in 1893, Peirce notes that through the course of history intellectual development has been uneven and often marked by "backward and barbarizing" movements. Even the early Christians were frequently barbaric, as in the case of St. John, who taught that some human beings would be resuscitated only so that they could be tortured for their sins. Peirce traces barbarism to "party spirit," which is his equivalent of Royce's "war-spirit": "One can understand that the early Christians were like men trying with all their might to climb a steep declivity of smooth wet clay; the deepest and truest element of their life, animating both heart and head, was universal love; but they were continually, and against their wills, slipping into a party spirit, every slip serving as a precedent, in a fashion but too familiar to every man."[26] Peirce does not explain why party spirit arises, just as he did not account for the prevalence in modern philosophy of feigned doubt. Both Cartesian doubt and party spirit are similar in that they separate the individual from the community, the first by a movement of thought that places the self at the center of experience and the second by an identification of the self with only one aspect of the world. The problem of the philosopher is overcoming radical separation and the *acedia* that shapes its mood, but the problem of social morality is tempering party spirit.

Peirce's most complete discussion of party spirit appears in his article, also published in 1893, "What Is Christian Faith?" He attempts here to trace religion to direct experience and to contrast "religious ideas," which are abstract and inert, to "religious phenomena," which are vital and sporadic. The necessary effort to make religion social causes "a degeneration in religion from a perception to a trust, from a trust to a belief, and a belief continually becoming more and more abstract." The "natural tendency" in religious development is to "the continual drawing tighter and tighter of the narrowing bounds of doctrine, with less and less attention to the living essence of religion." Here Peirce anticipates Unamuno's argument in *The Agony of Christianity* that the institutionalized church is incompatible with the freedom of Christian faith, but that institutions are essential to the social transmission of and, therefore, the material possibility for that faith. Peirce, however, does not espouse such a tragic and contradictory view, but states that "a narrow, little exclusive church is almost worse than none" and that "a great catholic church is wanted: . . . Discountenance as immoral all movements that exaggerate differences, or that go to make fellowship depend on formulas invented to exclude some Christians from communion with others."[27] Peirce's appeal for a "great catholic church" runs against his judgment that religious phenomena are sporadic and that the natural tendency of religion is to move from vivid perception to dull belief. Just as he did not acknowledge tragic existence in his critique of individualism, he does not do so in his polemic against party spirit and so can only note its ubiquity without incorporating it as an integral element in his theory of social life.

Peirce's inability or unwillingness to make a place for party spirit in his thought creates problems in his logic of science, which the other American classical philosophers deemed to be his greatest contribution. Peirce's defense of scientific method is founded on the principle that it is the only method that incorporates within its assumptions the idea of "fallibilism," the correction of beliefs through their social testing against experience. But, as Peirce observes, "the instinctive dislike of an undecided mind, exaggerated into a vague dread of doubt, makes men cling spasmodically to the views they already take." Peirce argues that fixing belief through "the method of tenacity" will be "unable to hold its ground" because "the social impulse is against it," but he acknowledges that tenacity can be collectivized as "the method of authority" and enforced through the coercive means of the state. He believes that in the long run the method of authority cannot hold its ground either and will cede, as he believes it has in modern times, first to the appeal to pure reason (the method of *a prioris*) and then to experimental method. Grounding his progressivism is his belief that human beings are directed toward reality ("the compulsion, the absolute constraint upon us to think otherwise than we have been thinking"), a belief that is based more deeply on the judgment that being is good, that life can be trusted, that all things are solidary with one another. But Peirce's synechism is at war with an equally profound realism or, perhaps, even a pessimism, which allows him to understand "the instinctive dislike of an undecided state of mind." Peirce's appeals for commitment to community and for willingness to revise opinions and welcome the contributions of all people of good will are placed in proper perspective only when they are interpreted as injunctions to overcome a natural entropy that is expressed sometimes in party spirit and sometimes in dull habit, boredom, and, ultimately, *acedia.* The tragic duality at the foundation of Peirce's thought is captured in his definition of human beings as imperfect logical animals who "are naturally more sanguine and hopeful than logic would justify."[28] Peirce, the first of the American philosophers to critique the idealistic thesis that human wishes find their necessary fulfillment in reality, was left with the duality implied by the critique. He insisted that the demands of the self were illogical but he did not succeed in demonstrating that they were unreal.

According to Royce, deliverance to the community was justified because efforts on its behalf were not futile or absurd. The apparent incompletions of human existence were, for Royce, resolved in the absolute life. Peirce did not have Royce's intellectual confidence in absolutism, but was sustained by a mystical vision that informed his philosophical thought from its very inception. The ease with which he experimented with the widest range of beliefs, the confidence that he had in shunting aside opinions that did not stand the test of experience, and the freedom for and receptivity to concrete life that are existential consequences of fallibilism all were made possible by the promise of communion. But, as Peirce noted, religious phenomena are sporadic. The American classical philosophers who succeeded Peirce had to think against the backdrop of the critique of idealism but without the mystical vision of synechism.

4

William James

C. S. Peirce's "acknowledgment" of the reality, though not the existence, of the absolute, as it was defined by Josiah Royce, allowed his life-commitment to fall within the context demarcated by nineteenth-century idealism. Both Peirce and Royce interpreted the absolute socially, as an unlimited community of minds in which the apparent discontinuities between individuals were overcome. They believed that the proper task of life-philosophy was to provide logical grounds for the objects of religious will, though they understood logic in different senses. Royce based his "absolute voluntarism" on an argument that claimed rational certainty, whereas Peirce grounded his defense of God's reality on a variety of what he considered to be plausible hypotheses. Both of them constructed their arguments atop more deeply held religious visions and experiences. The differences between their life-philosophies are minor, centering chiefly on the diverse qualities of their visions and on their styles of argument. With regard to the latter, Peirce contrasted traditional "argumentation," in which a chain of reasoning is no stronger than its weakest link, to his own use of "arguments," each one of which might be tenuous, but all of which together would be tight and strong like wires wound together in a cable. Peirce and Royce, however much they differed, were loyal to the great tradition of philosophy, for which life-commitments should be guided by objective knowledge of the nature of things. Royce believed that it was possible to know the very meaning of being through rational speculation, whereas Peirce held that the community of inquirers makes successive approximations to knowledge of reality, as fact is progressively sifted out from fantasy. But for both there was a close connection between knowledge and virtue.

The most significant breach in American classical philosophy is not that between Royce's absolute idealism and Peirce's pragmaticism, but between Peirce's and Royce's intellectualism, and William James's critique of the limits of the intellect in determining and justifying life-commitments. James became—particularly for Peirce, Royce, and John Dewey—the scandal of American life-philosophy, because his thought seemed to trifle with the philosophical vocation of loyalty to objective truth. Yet the other American classical philosophers did not attempt to deprecate his thought thoroughly. Each one of them, indeed, had reasons beyond intellectual debt to be grateful to James. Peirce was indebted to James for having credited him with founding pragmatism and for awakening a wide interest in his work. Royce was indebted to him for his very position at Harvard University. Dewey was, perhaps, in greater debt to James than the others, because James had awakened a wide public in America for philosophy, which extended beyond the academic community. Peirce and Dewey confined their critiques of James to noting the differences between a pragmatic method of ascertaining the meanings of concepts upon the structure of which "arguments concerning objective fact may hinge" (their interpretation of pragmatism), and a pragmatic theory of truth which held that ideas are true or false according to their experienced consequences (their assessment of James's intent).[1] Peirce also noted that the differences between his "pragmaticism" and James's "pragmatism" would hardly show up in everyday life and that their disagreements were far more profound in regard to how they understood "important questions of philosophy" concerning the infinite and the absolute. Peirce remarked that James had pressed some of his chief theses "further than the tether of their author would reach."[2] He referred here to his own acknowledgment of the reality of the absolute and to James's polemic against absolutism.

Royce's critique of James was far more stringent than those of Peirce and Dewey, perhaps because James leveled his most vigorous attacks against what he called the "block universe" presupposed by Royce's absolutism, and because Peirce and Dewey were associated with James in the general pragmatic movement of thought, which Peirce praised as a "living school." Royce considers James's life-philosophy in his 1913 work, *The Problem of Christianity*, in which he settled his philosophical accounts. He begins by stating that "there is one respect in which I am in full agreement with the spirit of pragmatism, as James defined it: . . . Any metaphysical thesis, if it has a meaning at all, is the expression of an attitude of the will of the one who asserts this thesis." From that point of agreement Royce goes on to critique the views of Hans Vaihinger, who substitutes for James as an object of attack. Royce summarizes Vaihinger's thesis as the proposition that "a philosophy is, in its essence, a resolution to treat the real world as if that world possessed certain characters, and as if our experience enabled us to verify these characters." Royce praises Vaihinger for having discerned that "our metaphysical interests are indeed interests in directing our will," but does not believe that the logical consequence of voluntarism is "a *mere* pragmatism." He contrasts to Vaihinger's pragmatism his own "absolute voluntarism," which is based on the principle that "there is one, and but one, general and decisive attitude of the will which is the right attitude, when we stand in presence of the universe, and when we undertake to choose how we propose to bear ourselves towards the world."[3] The "right attitude," according to Royce, is "essentially creative of its own realm of deeds," and each one of its "successes" has a "world-wide meaning." Each deed, for Royce, must be etched eternally in the absolute life. No achievement of goodness may be lost in Royce's cosmos. As was noted in the second chapter, this belief helped sustain Royce's will to overcome *acedia* and flowed, in part, from his vision of the holiness of each present moment.

William James would have responded to Royce's claim that there is one right attitude of the will by saying that perhaps there was one right attitude for Royce, the one that allowed him to live from day to day, but that others might be suffocated by the overbelief that gave Royce the confidence to strive. James argues along this line in his conclusion to *The Varieties of Religious Experience* where he characteristically defends a pluralism of life-commitments: "If an Emerson were forced to be a Wesley, or a Moody forced to be a Whitman, the total human consciousness of the divine would suffer. The divine can mean no single quality, it must mean a group of qualities, by being champions of which in alternation, different men may all find worthy missions."[4]

James's declaration of pluralism carries with it the implication that a James should not be forced to be a Royce, that, in a positive sense, all human beings should have the complete freedom to determine their own "worthy missions." James, however, should not be understood as the kind of subjectivist who argues that reasons are relative to groundless preferences, or that people have a right to whatever dispositions or attitudes they have in any present moment. James's pluralism and individualism are formed by a moral viewpoint. A good human life is not constituted by *any* mission, but by a worthy one. James, in fact, is as oriented toward community and solidarity as Royce and Peirce are, though his social vision emphasizes variety. Having made his plea for a pluralism of life-commitments, he continues by stating that each "attitude" is "a syllable in human nature's total message" and thus that "it takes the whole of us to spell the meaning out completely."[5] The difference between the philosophies of Peirce and Royce, and that of James is not collectivism versus individualism. All three thinkers attempt to do justice to the social and the personal aspects of human existence through idealized and universalistic concepts of community. James breaks with Royce and Peirce because his community is one of spiritual feeling whereas theirs is a community of truth-seekers. James's empiricism is deeply moral, being the most thoroughgoing critique of party spirit developed by the American classical philosophers. Each person should have freedom to determine a life-commitment because each one is different from the others and has, by virtue of that difference, a unique contribution to make to the interpretation of "human nature's total message."

The essential insight that informs James's thought is that life, grasped from within by an individual organism, is greater than any of its particular functions, including intellectual thought. James, then, is part of the movement of thought questioning idealism and mechanism that occurred at the turn of the twentieth century and was anticipated and guided by Arthur Schopenhauer and Friedrich Nietzsche. James's critique of intellectualism is grounded not in skepticism but in the vitalistic attempt to affirm concrete life and not to be contented with such symbolic reconciliations of its discontinuities and frustrations as the idea of the absolute. James differed with Peirce about the infinite and the absolute because he considered both of them to be abstractions that sublimated the vivid appreciation of finite good and diluted the bitterness of directly experienced evil. James's "world of pure experience," his "blooming and buzzing confusion," was an all-inclusive realm that contained both members of the pairs of pleasure and pain, good and evil, and success and failure, in whatever doses they happened to be experienced. The problem, of course, that someone who espouses such a comprehensive vitalism must confront is how the strip of direct experience that makes up a finite life can be affirmed wholeheartedly once it is known in its vital tensions and polarities, and particularly in its utter incompleteness, imperfection, and radical contingency. The problem of life-affirmation, which is inherent in vitalism, was the key concern of Nietzsche, who experienced the joy of "ascending life" and the despair and resentment of "declining life"; of Unamuno, who hungered for immortality and craved the peace of death; and of Dostoevsky, who experienced mystical union with life and consuming resentment against suffering. James falls within the line of modern vitalism, holding a place in American thought comparable to that held by Nietzsche in the history of German ideas and to Unamuno in Spanish thought.

Comprehensive vitalism, which James's thought represents in the discourse of American classical philosophy, does not hold fast to any specific religious vision such as Royce's experience of the holiness of each present moment or Peirce's vision of communion. For both of these thinkers one experience is so overpowering as to ground all of the others and to redeem, as Royce taught, even the pettiest of them. The comprehensive vitalist is not, to use James's term, so "healthy-minded" as to feel spontaneously the holiness of each moment or the unity of all beings. If, indeed, the comprehensive vitalist does experience moments that are consecrated or in which self is harmoniously unified with its surroundings, these moments are set alongside those that are permeated by what James calls "world-sickness." James's pluralism is anchored in a reflexive review of the broadest available range of experiences. In his chapter "The Sick Soul," in *The Varieties of Religious Experience*, he makes a declaration of pluralism against those who are "packed with healthy-mindedness." Even a person who has not experienced "sobering intervals" should, as a "reflecting being," generalize and "class his own lot with that of others; and, doing so, he must see that his escape is just a lucky chance and no essential difference." James's prescription for solidarity, therefore, is not commitment to others through the mediation of an idea, as it is for Royce and Peirce, but an effort at sympathy in which one's experience becomes more representative of human possibility. James is impressed by the radical contingency of finite life, which he cannot rationalize, and observes that the healthy-minded person "might just as well have been born to an entirely different fortune." And then he enters a characteristic moral reminder: "And then indeed the hollow security! What kind of a frame of things is it of which the best you can say is, 'Thank God, it has let me off clear this time!' "[6]

The reflexive review of experience, which is the method of comprehensive vitalism and which permits James to write about "varieties" of religious experience is, paradoxically, impelled in those who undertake it by an experience or recurrent experiences of "world-sickness." Nietzsche's stare into the abyss jolted him into recognition of the polar processes of ascension and decline of life. Unamuno's spiritual crisis, in which he experienced vital limitation and flirted with suicide, allowed him to affirm a paradoxical vision of human existence. Dostoevsky's prison experience, in which he was told that he would be executed, opened him to what he called the "breadth" of human character. James is no exception to the rule that comprehensive vitalism originates in world-sickness. Royce's methodical doubt, which carried him to the solipsism of the present moment, and Peirce's "real and living doubt," which directed him to explicate the "fixation of belief," are pale cognitive reflections of the radical separation involved in agonized doubting about existence. The root of existential doubting is not Royce's attempt to be "skeptical in a thorough-going way," which Peirce critiqued as meretricious posturing, nor is it Peirce's "irritation," which is a simple feeling among many others. Agonized doubting is based in fear, which runs much deeper, though it runs in the same psychological line as skepticism, which plays at fear, and as irritation, which, if it is examined and felt closely enough, and considered in the light of what it shows about life as a whole, can billow rapidly into fear. James is the only one of the American classical philosophers to have made the doubt about existence the basis of his life-philosophy. He called that existential doubting "panic fear."

James described his experience of panic fear in *The Varieties of Religious Experience* in the guise of a report given to him by a "sufferer." He writes of being in a "state of philosophic pessimism and general depression about my prospects," and of going into a dressing room to get something. In the room "there fell upon me without any warning, just as if it came out of the darkness, a horrible fear of my own existence." Simultaneously with the fear James remembered an "epileptic patient" whom he had seen in an asylum. The patient sat all day on a bench "moving nothing but his black eyes and looking absolutely nonhuman." The image of the patient fused with the fear and James experienced the radical contingency of existence: "*That shape am I*, I felt, potentially. Nothing that I possess can defend me against that fate, if the hour for it should strike for me as it struck for him." James reports that having reached his judgment "it was as if something hitherto solid within my breast gave way entirely, and I became a mass of quivering fear." In the days that succeeded the experience he felt "a horrible dread at the pit of my stomach" and "a sense of the insecurity of life." He became "sympathetic with the morbid feelings of others" and could not understand how he had previously been able to live "so unconscious of that pit of insecurity beneath the surface of life." James reports that he believed his "experience of melancholia" to have "a religious bearing," because he felt that he would have grown insane had he not "clung to scripture-texts like 'The eternal God is my refuge,' etc. . . ."[7]

James did not provide an existential analysis of what he called "the worst kind of melancholy," but one can be derived from his description of the experience. The experience has two facets that, though James does not do so, may be sharply distinguished from one another. The first of them is the "horrible fear" of his own existence, which is the acute form of *acedia,* an immobilization of the will to live. Panic fear in its purest form renders the one who suffers it unable to transcend the present moment, incapable of forming any project demanding self-control. The sufferer is at the mercy of autonomic responses to stimuli and verges on becoming a "mass of quivering fear." Panic fear is the failure of practicality, which means lacking the ability to affirm oneself as an actor in the world. The fear of existence, as Jean-Paul Sartre teaches, is a fear of taking hold of oneself through a concrete commitment. It is the mockery of deliverance to any project, because it reveals all projects to be merely conventional constructions. The second facet of James's experience is the image of the epileptic patient which arose simultaneously with the panic fear. For an existential analysis this aspect of James's experience does not reveal a fundamental structure of life, but is the result of a protective psychological mechanism that allowed James to limit and define the all-consuming panic fear by giving it a specific object and by diverting it from dread to guilt. James's way of containing his panic fear, thus, was to identify himself with someone who was perpetually immobilized and then to make his present dread a fear of a possible future by imagining himself as an epileptic. The flight of James from existential dread was unconscious and, of course, was not insincere. However, the diversion of panic fear of the present to fear of a possible future in the present helped to determine the supremacy of moral concerns in James's later thought.

The succeeding stages of James's experience are determined by the fixation of the panic fear, which in itself is utterly groundless (the fear suddenly "fell upon" him "without any warning, just as if it came out of the darkness"), on the image of the epileptic. The fear and the image fuse, and the synthesis created is judged by James to reveal the radical contingency of existence and the insecurity of life. He saves himself from growing "really insane," which would mean, presumably, becoming swallowed up by and lost in his fear, by clinging to scriptural passages in which God is a refuge and helper of the weak. The lesson James learned from his experience was one of humility, dependency, and vulnerability. He carried his initial identification with the helpless (the epileptic patient) to an appeal to the God who cares for the helpless. In the light of the moral direction in which he resolved his panic fear James's revulsion against the sentiment "Thank God, it has let me off clear this time!" is intelligible. He escaped from the deepest radical separation, existential dread, by delivering himself to solidarity with the suffering ("the experience has made me sympathetic with the morbid feelings of others ever since"). James's doubt, indeed, was far more profound than that of either Royce or Peirce, but he resolved it in the same way that they did theirs.

James's experience of panic fear was preceded by a period of two years in which he suffered a "suicidal depression" and fought "an inward battle to continue living." It was another two years after sensing the pit of insecurity beneath personal experience before he recovered a relatively stable will to live. During his fight for recovery James felt the boredom and distaste for life most commonly associated with *acedia* and, as Clebsch notes, "began saving himself from acedia, a feat traditionally held impossible."[8] In chapter 21 of his *The Principles of Psychology* James described a "pathological state which is as far removed from doubt as from belief, and which some may consider the proper contrary of the latter state of mind: . . . I refer to the feeling that everything is hollow, unreal, dead." Those who suffer from such melancholy, as James's correspondence shows he did, complain that "nothing is believed in by them as it used to be, and that all sense of reality is fled from life."[9]

James could not overcome his melancholy solely through his solidarity with the suffering. He resorted not only to acting with his will, but also to believing with it, and described at the end of chapter 21 of *The Principles* what Clebsch calls the "private ritual" of his spirituality. According to James, will can lead on to belief in an object: *"we need only in cold blood* act *as if the thing in question were real, and keep acting as if it were real, and it will become real."*[10] This application of the method of tenacity, of making "a little sacrifice" to "God" and "Duty" every day, became the basis of James's later philosophical discussions of belief. In 1879, about ten years after he experienced panic fear, James began teaching philosophy at Harvard and published his first major contribution to life-philosophy, "The Sentiment of Rationality." In this work, as in those concerning life-commitment that succeed it, James provides a rationalized account of how he overcame panic fear. The rationalization becomes stabilized and rigid in the central expression of American life-philosophy, "The Will to Believe."

The pattern of James's philosophical project is similar to that of Royce. The experience of panic fear was, though involuntary, a withdrawal into the wilderness of the mind. From this sojourn in a terrifying wilderness James emerged with a radically altered vision of the cosmos. Royce's drama of the wanderer, of course, is sublimated and domesticated. The wilderness is one of cognitive doubt and the reward for suffering is a "soul-stirring vision of the truth" which is given as a gift to the ongoing community by the philosopher. James's drama, in contrast, is not sublimated. His

wilderness is one of existential dread and his suffering is unre-
deemed by any knowledge that justifies it. James does not have a
gift for the community as a whole, because his awareness of "the
pit of insecurity beneath the surface of life" prevents him from affirming confidently that the city and the wilderness are ruled by
the same god. James's "worthy mission" is to defend the rights of
the "sick soul" to find any way to live from one day to the next, as
long as that way does not destroy the solidarity of human beings
with one another. Having confronted his own deficient will to live
in the experience of panic fear and having overcome that fear
through a desperate clinging to religious formulations, James
made the core of his life-philosophy a "justification of faith" as a
means to the continuance of present life. James was careful to
note frequently that he did not wish to lead the healthy-minded
into world-sickness, but only to remind them that others did suffer and deserved permission to seek their own cures. Here James
differed from Unamuno, another vitalist who challenged the "in-
quisition of science." Unamuno's project, though it contained a
justification of faith, was primarily to draw people into world-sickness by "pouring salt" on the wounds that they tried so assiduous-
ly to heal. He called the healthy-minded "cultural men" who ex-
changed the fullness of their personalities for social reassurances.
James was less certain of the superiority of the sick soul than
Unamuno was. The latter, who tried but was unable to exert a will
to believe, took the offensive against the "cultured despisers" of religion. James, who was squarely within the American tradition,
did not set himself against the community, but fought a defensive
battle.

The primary weapon in James's defensive battle was a new conception of philosophy which he unveiled in "The Sentiment of Rationality." The essay is a response to the question that is raised in
its first sentence: "What is the task which philosophers set themselves to perform; and why do they philosophize at all?"[11] James
responds that philosophers "desire to attain a conception of the
frame of things which shall on the whole be more rational than
that somewhat chaotic view which everyone by nature carries
about with him under his hat." Thus, James defines the philosopher's task in a way similar to Royce and Peirce, both of whom
held that their special task was to construct and defend a worldview. However, whereas Royce sought his conception of the frame

of things in speculative reason and Peirce searched for his among the methods and hypotheses of experimental science, James raised the prior question of how the philosopher is able to recognize the rationality of a worldview. His answer is that rationality is a "sentiment" which is identified "by certain subjective marks" with which it affects the knower.

The most obvious of these subjective marks, according to James, is the pleasure that accompanies finding that "a chaos of facts is the expression of a single underlying fact: . . . The passion for parsimony, for economy of means in thought, is the philosophic passion *par excellence;* and any character or aspect of the world's phenomena which gathers up their diversity into monotony will gratify that passion, and in the philosopher's mind stand for that essence of things compared with which all their other determinations may by him be overlooked." James, however, does not permit the "theoretic need" and the "philosophic passion," which are merely aspects of concrete life, to determine the "sentiment of rationality." The "passion for simplification," which informs what James later called "monism" and the "block universe," is counterbalanced by "the passion for distinguishing" which informs the "pluralistic universe." However, even if a conception of the frame of things were constructed that combined unity and diversity harmoniously, James is not satisfied that it would be rational. He notes that "our mind is so wedded to the process of seeing an *other* beside every item of its experience, that when the notion of an absolute datum is presented to it, it goes through its usual procedure and remains pointing at the void beyond, as if in that lay further matter for contemplation."[12] The idea of the void is a product of the spontaneous functioning of the mind, which limits satisfaction with even the most harmonious synthesis of the one and the many. James argues that only "when the conception of the universe as a unique fact is nearest its perfection" does "the ontological wonder-sickness" arise "in its extremest form." Ontological wonder-sickness, which, according to James, is the inability to suppress the question "Why was there anything but nonentity; why just this universal datum and not another?" arises in the shadow of idealism. It is the logical antithesis to absolutism based on "the blighting breath of the ultimate Why?"

James's description of ontological wonder-sickness recalls the entire philosophical project of Martin Heidegger, who posed the question of metaphysics in exactly the same way as James did before him, but who devoted his life as a thinker to making sure that the question was not suppressed. Heidegger, of course, interpreted the meaning or import of the question differently than James did, holding that the void was not merely an artifact of abstract thinking but a concrete experience that arises in moments of dread. James, who experienced panic fear and apprehended "the pit of insecurity beneath the surface of life," could have broken the path that Heidegger attempted to clear, but, instead, he covered over the nothingness of dread with the idea of logical negation. This was the first and determinative step that James took toward rationalizing panic fear and justifying faith as an escape from it. It is at this point, where James makes a cognitive substitution for dread, that the possibility for an American existentialism was lost. Rather than remaining close to the lived experience of ontological insecurity, which radically separates the self from its ordinary mundanity, James uses the idea of radical contingency to show that theoretical reason does not satisfy the sentiment of rationality. If for every absolute datum there is just as absolute a negation, then "the bottom of being is left logically opaque to us, as something which we simply come upon and find, and about which (if we wish to act) we should pause and wonder as little as possible."[13]

James wishes, above all, to act. He remarks that in "moments of energetic living we feel as if there were something diseased and contemptible, yea vile, in theoretic grubbing and brooding." The philosopher is, in "the eye of healthy sense," at best "a learned fool." Yet James also notes, undermining the unilateral visions of Royce and Peirce, that the "mystical method" of walling out "the ultimate irrationality which the head ascertains" has "lacked universality, being available for few persons and at few times, and even in these being apt to be followed by fits of reaction and dryness." Such "fits of reaction and dryness" are experiences of *acedia* in which the zest for living is lost, indifference replaces the sense of importance, and the self is radically separated from life-commitments and is unable to mount any demanding or extensive projects. James, who experienced a "horrible fear" of his own existence and then a long period of *acedia*, did not, at least, succumb to the reaction formation of positive mysticism. He observes that "if men should agree that the mystical method is a subterfuge without logical pertinency, a plaster but no cure, and that the idea of nonentity can never be exorcised, empiricism will be the ultimate philosophy."[14] The ground, then, of James's empiricism, of his radical interpretation of experience, is ontological wonder. From the viewpoint of "purely theoretic rationality" existence "will be a brute fact to which as a whole wonder shall rightly cleave, but remain eternally unsatisfied." This is James's compromise with his existential insight. By sublimating it to the plane of "theoretic rationality" he does not deny it, but he tames it sufficiently to allow him to act, which means to live. He does not go over to the side of the mystics, such as Royce and Peirce, who attempt to "wall out the ultimate irrationality," but he puts his shoulder to the wheel in the practical life, along with all the other healthy-minded people.

There is an abrupt break in "The Sentiment of Rationality" after the discussion of ontological wonder-sickness. James begins the new section by observing that if "impediments" to "mental function" arise in the theoretic sphere, they might be avoided "if the stream of mental action should leave that sphere betimes and pass into the practical." The practical sphere is governed by an entirely different question than that which defines the theoretic realm. The "radical question of life" is "whether this be at bottom a moral or an unmoral universe." From the theoretic viewpoint this question has already been answered. The universe is, for the sensitive observer of life, unmoral, because the ultimate irrationality of the datum of experience cannot be suppressed. Heidegger, who waged a polemic against what he called "moral existentialism," drew the consequences of the separation of the practical from the theoretic realm by eliminating teleological reasoning from metaphysics and by analyzing practical life on its own terms, without the support of a conception of the frame of things. James did not break Heidegger's path, but, instead, retreated to the traditional project of constructing a worldview to guide practice. His worldview, of course, did not claim theoretic rationality, but did claim practical rationality, in the sense that it promoted, at least for James, the "feeling of the sufficiency of the present moment," the "absence of all need to explain it, account for it, or justify it." In order to affirm life James had to believe in a moral universe.

James had anticipated the structure of his reasoning in "The Sentiment of Rationality" in his reflections on his spiritual crisis which he placed in his diary in 1870. Gay Wilson Allen suggests that the death of his cousin Minny Temple in 1870 probably brought on James's experience of panic fear. On March 22, 1870, James wrote in his diary: "Minny, your death makes me feel the nothingness of all our egotistic fury. The inevitable release is sure; wherefore take our turn kindly whatever it contain. Ascend to some partnership with fate, & since tragedy is at the heart of us, go to meet it, work it into our ends, instead of dodging it all our days, and being run down by it at last." Here James is still on the theoretical side of experience, remaining close to the moment of ontological insecurity and trying to fashion an attitude toward existence that will allow him to live from day to day in the presence of tragedy. He is attempting to incorporate death into life, to tolerate it inwardly rather than to evade it: he approaches Heidegger's understanding that human existence is being-toward-death and that authentic existence is resolute decision in full awareness of one's finitude. By April 30, 1870, however, James had read some writings of Charles Renouvier and became convinced that he could posit an autonomous practical standpoint: "I think yesterday was a crisis in my life. I finished the first part of Renouvier's 2nd Essay and saw no reason why his definition of free will— 'the sustaining of a thought *because I choose to* when I might have other thoughts' —need be the definition of an illusion. At any rate I will assume for the present—until next year—that it is no illusion. My first act of free will shall be to believe in free will." James resolves to "voluntarily cultivate the feeling of moral freedom" and to "care little for speculation." He abandons the attempt to build a life in the constant awareness of nothingness, to build the revelations of the wilderness into existence in the city, and decides instead to "posit life, (the real, the good) in the self governing resistance of the ego to the world."[15] James's "posit" remains the dominant theme of his life-philosophy through the rest of his career, but the theme of inward tolerance persists, as will be made evident in analysis of "The Will to Believe," as a counterpoint.

James's moral universe is a "conception of the frame of things," an "over-belief," which includes objective evil, so that our actions to overcome *acedia* make a difference; and a tendency toward the victory of goodness, so that those actions are not in vain. This sophisticated and paradoxical response to idealism and skepticism is, according to James, the belief that is best adapted to promote a strenuous life of devotion to a worthy mission. In a later essay, "The Moral Philosopher and the Moral Life," published in 1891, James argues that "the stable and systematic moral universe for which the ethical philosopher asks is fully possible only in a world where there is a divine thinker with all-enveloping demands." He bases this claim on the ground that "our attitude towards concrete evils is entirely different in a world where we believe there are none but finite demanders, from what it is in one where we joyously face tragedy for an infinite demander's sake."[16] The justification of faith because it promotes the strenuous effort within society to overcome finite evils is a long way from the desperate experience of clinging to scriptural texts in order to avoid going mad. James makes the judgment here that human beings will not deliver themselves wholeheartedly to one another's care unless they believe that there are "all-enveloping demands." That which originally makes up for a deficient will to live has been transformed into a doctrine encouraging us to "joyously face tragedy."

James experienced the American philosopher's agony of reconciling the wilderness and the city more acutely than either Royce or Peirce did. The wilderness into which James was thrown against his will, when he experienced panic fear, had no God. He was the only one of the group of American classical philosophers to be formed by the experience that led Nietzsche to proclaim his death of God decree. James, therefore, did not have the task of trying to show that the wilderness and the city are ruled by the same God. His mission was to seek out God elsewhere than in the wilderness. His experience of panic fear blocked him from the possibility of returning to the city with a "soul-stirring vision of the truth." He had, in fact, to return to the city empty-handed. James reports that he overcame his panic fear only by clinging to scriptural texts. He was not saved from madness, then, by reason or by faith, but by the sheer exertion of will. His will, of course, was focused on repeating passages from the Bible, but he could not be sure that the particular object of attention that allowed him to gain control of himself was any more than an accidental association. James carried back from the wilderness merely the knowledge that he had been able, at least that one time, to summon the will to live. He was determined not to return a second time if he could help it, and so pledged himself to the city.

The split between theoretical reasoning and practical reason-

ing, which is opened up in "The Sentiment of Rationality," is a reflection of the deeper rupture between a terrible wilderness and a
social world that offers the only escape from that wilderness.
James could not deliver himself to society through an intellectual
ideal, as did Royce and Peirce, but he had to seek his own salvation
through obedience to the God of the city, who appears in the form
of a "divine thinker with all-enveloping demands." James had no
mystical vision beyond the reach of society to sustain his participation in it and to offer as a gift and contribution to the lives of others. For all of their devotion to community, Peirce and Royce had
an independence of judgment secured both by their universal
ideals and by their deeper visions of the goodness of being. James
had to affirm the God of the city against the wilderness, which accounts for his recourse to practical reasoning. The vocation of the
American philosopher is to contribute to the realization of a moral
community by teaching others to make ethical commitments.
James attempted to fulfill that vocation in the only way he could,
by promoting those ideas that would encourage moral participation. His worthy mission involved the twin tasks of instilling "sick
souls" with the courage to devote themselves to the common life
and of convincing the "healthy-minded" to tolerate and even to
appreciate the need for faith of those who suffered from "world-
sickness."

James's central contribution to American life-philosophy, "The
Will to Believe," is best understood in the light of his sympathy for
those who suffered from "world-sickness." The essay is explicitly a
"justification of faith, a defense of our right to a believing attitude
in religious matters, in spite of the fact that our merely logical intellect may not have been coerced." The project of justifying faith,
which led Karl Jaspers to call James's pragmatism a "cheap optimism" and a "blind confidence in the extant confusion," is given a
more profound moral basis by understanding it as an admonition
directed to the healthy-minded and a boost of encouragement for
the sick souls. The essence of James's argument is that *our pas-
sional nature not only lawfully may, but must, decide an option between propositions, whenever it is a genuine option that cannot by
its nature be decided on intellectual grounds.*" According to James,
a genuine option is "living" (each alternative makes some appeal
to belief), "forced" (there is no "standing place" outside of the alternatives), and "momentous" (the opportunity is unique). As long

as the option between religious belief and unbelief is live for a person, James can show that it is forced and momentous. He defines the essence of religion as the two affirmations that "the best things are the more eternal things, the overlapping things, the things in the universe that throw the last stone, so to speak, and say the final word"; and that "we are better off even now if we believe (the) first affirmation to be true."[17] The heart of religion for James, then, is the proposition that being is good, the same proposition upon which Royce based his absolutism and Peirce grounded his fallibilism. All three of these thinkers fall into the Platonic tradition through their acceptance of this proposition and through their belief that it is the basis of life-philosophy. James differs from the two others only in identifying the proposition that being is good with practical rationality rather than with theoretic reason, and in arguing that affirming the proposition brings benefits in the present. For James, as for the other American classical philosophers, except Santayana, the vision of a moralized cosmos provides human beings with the confidence to participate in cooperative endeavors with others. James is merely more tough-minded than Royce, Peirce, or Dewey because he does not believe that the moralized cosmos can be demonstrated or even supported by theoretical reasoning.

The culmination of "The Will to Believe" is James's expression of his over-belief. Having defined the essence of religion as the belief that "the best things are the more eternal things," he notes that "the more perfect and more eternal aspect of the universe is represented in our religions as having personal form."[18] For the religious vision "the universe is no longer a mere *It* to us, but a *Thou*." James derives from the personalized interpretation of the cosmos the idea that "any relation that may be possible from person to person" might be possible from a human being to God. Perhaps, he remarks, religion makes its most direct appeal to "our own active good-will" and we must meet "the hypothesis half-way" if we are to verify it. In such a case the relation of the person to God would be patterned after a moral relation among human beings in which each one must trust the other in order to preserve the freedom and good will of both. The idea of a God to whom we relate as we relate to one another is a humanization of religion. The limited God who will not be revealed unless met half-way is the God of the city moralized, not the absolute of the wilderness domesticated.

James, indeed, models his account of religious belief explicitly on moral experience. Having argued that in scientific inquiry, where there is no forced option, "the dispassionately judicial intellect with no pet hypothesis, saving us, as it does, from dupery at any rate, ought to be our ideal," he goes on to assert that in contrast moral questions "immediately present themselves as questions whose solution cannot wait for sensible proof." Moral experience, for James, concerns what is good or what would be good if it existed, and is a matter of the heart. Even science "consults her heart when she lays it down that the infinite ascertainment of fact and correction of false belief are the supreme goods for man." Moral skepticism, in James's view, "can no more be refuted or proved by logic than intellectual scepticism can." The core of the moral standpoint is not certainty or persuasive evidence that value commitments make a difference for the character of experience, but trust in their transforming power. Just as one person wins another's love, not by waiting for objective evidence of affection, but by an active movement of trust and expectation, so "a social organism of any sort whatever, large or small, is what it is because each member proceeds to his own duty with a trust that the other members will simultaneously do theirs." Society, for this interpretation, is a creation of risk and commitment rather than a process that goes forward independently of individual will: "Wherever a desired result is achieved by the co-operation of many independent persons, its existence as a fact is a pure consequence of the percursive faith in one another of those immediately concerned." In ordinary social life individuals may mask from their awareness the importance of will in constituting predictable and solidary relations, but James brings out clearly that society is a fact that is not brought into being "unless a preliminary faith exists in its coming."[19]

If, as James suggests, the relation of humans to God is social, then there is a sense in which God, though not a simple creation of human faith, is brought out of relative isolation and enriched by individual believers. James notes that "although in one sense we are passive portions of the universe, in another we show a curious autonomy, as if we were small active centres on our own account." Part of the contribution of the individual's activity to the course of things may be through belief. James alludes to the "feeling, forced on us we know not whence, that by obstinately believing that there are gods (although not to do so would be so easy both for our logic and our life), we are doing the universe the deepest service we can," and notes that this feeling "seems part of the living essence of the religious hypothesis."[20] Here James approaches the position of Nikos Kazantzakis—that human beings are the "saviors of god" through their efforts to overcome their despair. God becomes in James's conception a partner in a cooperative endeavor, a fellow citizen in the universe.

A moralized God of the city, of whom individual human beings are the saviors, can accommodate unbelievers. James does not conclude his discussion of life-commitment, as Royce did, with an affirmation that "there is one, and but one, general and decisive attitude of the will which is the right attitude." More important to James than any consensus on ultimate commitment is the moral imperative to avoid party spirit. He acknowledges that no intellectual logic prohibits a person from rejecting religious belief as he defines it and that only individuals can judge whether belief is life-sustaining in the present. Practical reasoning is not coercive, but permissive. Both the believer and the unbeliever act, taking their lives in their hands: "No one of us ought to issue vetoes to the other, nor should we bandy words of abuse. We ought, on the contrary, delicately and profoundly to respect one another's mental freedom: then only shall we bring about the intellectual republic; then only shall we have that spirit of inner tolerance without which all our outer tolerance is soulless, and which is empiricism's glory; then only shall we live and let live, in speculative as well as in practical things."[21]

James's greatest contribution to American life-philosophy is not his justification of faith or his image of a moralized God of the city, but his idea of an intellectual republic, which is the glory of empiricism, not the crown of faith. In the thought of William James a decisive shift occurs in American life-philosophy which is only imperfectly expressed in his obvious installation of God as the object of practical reason. Once belief in God is made belief in "a conception of the frame of things" it is neither a rational necessity nor even a plausible hypothesis but an aid to living in the present, to feeling "the sufficiency of the present moment." If it does not embrace life, belief should be abandoned. Of course, this position inverts the traditional idea that human beings are relative to God, but its implications go further than that. Not only is God humanized, but social morality is made supreme over religion and independent of it. A moralized God of the city no longer rules the city but, in a sense, becomes one of its citizens, subject not to the demands of practical rationality but to the intrinsic morality of empiricism. James, of course, did not work out the implications of his declaration of an "intellectual republic." He spent the greatest part of his life as a thinker barring any of the doors that led back to the experience of panic fear and discharging the American philosophical vocation of being a religio-moral teacher. The project that occupied his attention was the justification of faith through the construction of experimental over-beliefs which became ever more generous as he grew older, approximating more closely to, but never becoming identical with the image of an intellectual republic that is the "last word" of his most famous essay. James was a transitional thinker who defended the religious faith in strenuous deliverance to the community, which was the soul of early American classical philosophy, but who defended that faith as one alternative among others in an intellectual republic. James's idea of a "spirit of inner tolerance," which is the antidote to the war-spirit, is the moral basis of his method of reflective review of experience. It is the purely moral vision that he is able to express when he is not in flight from panic fear but has achieved a spontaneous confidence that allows him to affirm life as a whole.

The high point in American life-philosophy is reached in the thought of William James. If his justification of faith is separated from his insight into existence, two visions remain, one of them ontological and the other moral. The ontological vision is encapsulated in the speculation that if people should agree that the idea of nonentity can never be exorcised, empiricism will be the ultimate philosophy. The moral vision is expressed in the statement that the spirit of inner tolerance is empiricism's glory. That the idea of nonentity be accepted as one of two antithetical ultimates accommodates the experience of panic fear, in which the "pit of insecurity" is revealed beneath the surface of life. That a spirit of inner tolerance be cultivated implements the moral vision that each attitude toward existence is a "syllable in human nature's total message." The core of nonentity is panic fear and that of inner tolerance is concrete appreciation of one's relativity with regard to others. James failed in his attempt to make the God of the city substitute, unaided, for the God of the wilderness. But in his constant efforts he revealed possibilities that reach beyond the religious problematic of American classical philosophy. The two great figures who succeeded James—Santayana and Dewey—did not separate the ontological and the moral, purifying each, and setting them in tension with each other, but constructed new moral ontologies, replacing a fallen idealism with naturalism.

5

John Dewey

The sharpest challenge that William James directed against the idealistic philosophies of Josiah Royce and C. S. Peirce was his critique of mystical union in "The Sentiment of Rationality," in which he argued that the method of walling out the judgments that "existence is a brute fact," and that "the idea of nonentity can never be exorcised," lacked universality and stability. James's suspicion of monistic ontologies and his hypothesis of a pluralistic universe were based not only on an embracement of the variety of lived experience, but more deeply on the insight that the idea of nonentity implies radical discontinuity. The impulse to mystical unity is fulfilled in such visions as Royce's of the completion of all incompletions in the absolute life and Peirce's of the communion of all beings in being. Essential to mystical vision is what Peirce called "synechism," the idea of continuity, which excludes radical separation. In contrast to mysticism, the idea of a pluralistic universe implies at least the possibility that some beings are separated from others and that, therefore, there are gaps in the cosmos. The depth levels of James's thought can be traced from a superficial contrast of the impulse to unity and the impulse to variety, through the insight that variety implies discontinuity, and to the judgment that discontinuity implies the idea of nonentity. Beneath this theoretical dualism, of course, lies the experience of "panic fear," which provides the motive power for "ontological wonder-sickness."

James's escape from ontological wonder-sickness, from doubt

about the meaning of being, was to transfer the idea of continuity from the sphere of "theoretic" contemplation to that of practical reasoning. Rather than grounding practicality on a vision of the community of being, as Peirce and Royce did, James made continuity an idea to stimulate self-overcoming by declaring the essence of religion to be the belief, not the experienced fact or rational idea, that "the best things are the more eternal things, the overlapping things." James's rigid and uncompromising split between theoretic contemplation and practical reasoning created a scandal in American philosophy which the succeeding generation of thinkers, dominated by John Dewey and George Santayana, attempted to rectify or at least to cover up. James, the "sick soul," had preached a variant of "positive thinking" that was so sophisticated and profound as to make him a "knight of faith" in the sense of Sören Kierkegaard. He revealed that the essence of Royce's and Peirce's life-philosophies was a mystical form of party spirit in which "the ultimate irrationality which the head ascertains" is walled out of awareness. James's scandal was to have claimed that theoretical contemplation cannot achieve the knowledge that being is good and that the way to goodness lies in promoting life by whatever beliefs are the most appropriate. He had imperiled the principle that knowledge is virtue by substituting for it the virtue of belief.

James's starting point was neither the transcendental and comprehensive doubting of Royce nor the severely limited "real and living doubt" of Peirce, but, most profoundly the existential insecurity of panic fear, and, as a cognitive reflection of fear, the wondering doubt expressed in the question: "Why was there anything but nonentity; why just this universal datum and not another?" As Heidegger shows in *Being and Time*, wondering doubt is a direct entry way to the existential doubt of dread. Once the question of the meaning of being has been raised within a philosophical tradition it must become the theme for reflection and be encountered, repeatedly, in its existential dimension, or it must be walled out of awareness by some vision or doctrine that promotes the judgment that things are as they should be, or, at least, that human beings should accept "just this universal datum" as it is presented to them. Naturalism, which is the third and final phase of American classical philosophy, is shaped by the project of showing that human beings should accept "just this universal datum" as it is pre-

sented to them, that they should resign themselves to the "ultimate irrationality which the head ascertains."

American classical philosophy moves from an idealistic and
mystical phase in which confidence in the goodness of being is
proclaimed, through a dualistic, empirical, and vitalistic phase in
which being and goodness are held apart and set into tension
with one another, and on to a naturalistic phase in which reconciliation with being is sought, although being cannot be affirmed
to be good either through vision or through reason. Of the two
great American naturalisms, Dewey's counsels that the world in
which we live be made better to the greatest extent possible, and
Santayana's invites people to appreciate to the fullest the goodness that being provides. The wider import of these philosophies
of resignation to a lack of certainty about any ultimate meaning for
life can be understood against the background of James's challenge and of his scandal. American philosophy lost its innocence
when James presented his challenge to any rationalization or in-
tuitive justification of the "universal datum," "pure experience."
Neither Dewey nor Santayana attempted to respond to the challenge by mounting a new defense of idealism and, with it, of Christianity. James had effectively brought Nietzsche's death of God
decree to America, though he attempted to avoid its extreme consequences through his appeal to the notion of a finite God. But the
great naturalists did not accept the will to believe as a solution to
the failure of theoretic contemplation. They attempted to unite
the self to its world through the all-comprehensive category of
nature.

The naturalisms of Dewey and Santayana are made possible by
an avoidance of both wondering doubt and existential insecurity.
Dewey and Santayana skirt the issue of ontological wonder-sickness by appealing to the more superficial forms of doubting undertaken by Royce and Peirce. Dewey recurs to Peirce's "real and
living doubt" as the basis of his experimentalism, and Santayana
repeats Royce's journey to the solipsism of the present moment.
Dewey, however, does not, as Peirce did, construct a world picture
or conception of the "frame of things" that is consistent with the
conclusions of the experimental sciences, but accepts the "universal datum" as it is presented to him. Similarly, Santayana does
not model a vision of an eternal cosmos on the solipsism of the
present moment, but embraces each moment just as it is, as an ul-

timate datum, and posits an "animal faith" in continuity. The hall-mark of both naturalisms is acceptance of the thesis that existence is contingent and that meaning appears within it rather than in-forming it and providing its very structure. Neither the regulative idealism of Peirce, in which infinity and the absolute are held to be real, though nonexistent, nor the constitutive idealism of Royce, in which the absolute life is eternal, survived James's proclamation of the radical contingency of existence. The new moral ontologies were chastened and sober, and critical of any confidence in being sustained by idealization of some of its possibilities, even when the ideal was held as a hypothesis of practical reasoning. Both Dewey and Santayana forebore from introducing the idea of eter-nity into their thought, adopting the thesis that existence is temporal. Yet they stopped short of James's radical thesis that "ex-perience leans on itself." For Dewey, philosophy reflects upon "experienced existence," and for Santayana, the "realm of matter" is the support for objective truth. They were enabled to limit their doubting by putting a new natural foundation for experience in place of the old ideal one.

The heart of Dewey's thought is that doubting and questioning arise within a common-sense world, which is taken for granted by its thinking inhabitants, and that these processes are most appro-priately resolved by reconstruction of the world to alter the prob-lematic situations that cause them. Dewey states his position on the proper scope of doubting in his essay, "The Existence of the External World as a Logical Problem," in which he argues that "there is no problem, logically speaking, of the existence of an ex-ternal world," because "the very attempt to state the problem in-volves a self-contradiction." In brief, Dewey's claim is that in order to doubt the existence of an external world the existence of such a world must be presupposed. Addressing the reduction of experi-ence to a solipsism of the present moment, he asks how "even the act of being aware is describable as 'momentary,' " and responds that he "knows of no way of so identifying it except by discover-ing that it is delimited in a time continuum." Thus, he concludes that "it is surely superfluous to bother about *inference* to 'other times.' " The other times are "assumed in stating the question"; a supposed inference to them depends upon their already having been presupposed as elements of a common-sense world. Dewey holds, therefore, that "what is doubtful is not the existence of the world but the validity of certain customary yet inferential beliefs about things in it: . . . It is not the common-sense *world* which is doubtful, or which is inferential, but *common-sense* as a complex of beliefs about specific things and relations *in* the world."[1] According to Dewey, then, genuine doubt is, as it was also for Peirce, a state that refers to certain problems that appear within the course of life, rather than to the problematicity of life itself. In order to take this position Dewey restricts his critique to the methodical doubting associated with transcendental philosophy and does not address either wondering doubt or existential insecurity.

Dewey is, indeed, correct that the "problem of the existence of the external world" presupposes its own solution. However, as Royce and Santayana show, it is possible to bring the critique of knowledge to the point at which only a present datum can be affirmed with certainty. The affirmation of the particular datum as datum and as present presupposes, of course, a world of various data and a time perspective of past-present-future in which they appear; but those presuppositions do not violate the integrity of the lived present as an irreducible datum. There is a difference between the solipsism of the present moment as experienced and the affirmation of the solipsism of the present moment as the terminus of the transcendental critique of knowledge. Santayana made this difference the basis of his distinction between the "order of evidence," in which the present datum is ultimate, and the "order of genesis," in which the present datum is judged to be an aspect of a spatio-temporal world process. Dewey attempts to evade Santayana's distinction by adding to his logical critique, "as a hypothesis," that "even the most rudimentary conscious experience contains within itself the element of suggestion or expectation," which would mean that the perspective of a past-present-future beyond the lived present is constitutive of the lived present. This hypothesis is required to challenge the solipsism of the present moment in the order of evidence, but Dewey admits that "one may be unwilling to concede" it.

Having declared the problem of the existence of the external world to be a pseudo-problem involving a self-contradiction, Dewey's great philosophical embarrassment became the need to account for why previous thinkers had erred so radically. The most ambitious attempt that he made to explain the vanity of earlier philosophical speculation was in *The Quest for Certainty: A Study of the Relation of Knowledge and Action,* published in 1929. Dewey's general argument in this work is that the great tradition in Western philosophy has been motivated by a search for absolute knowledge. However, according to Dewey, certainty about the meaning of being cannot be achieved, whereas provisional knowledge gained through the methods of experimental science can be attained and can be used to transform the world so that human life is more productive of goodness. Thus, Dewey's project is to defend a search for "reasonable security," guided by the use of experimental method in all phases of life, as a substitute for the traditional "quest for certainty."

Dewey begins his discussion with a general thesis about human nature: "Man who lives in a world of hazards is compelled to seek for security."[2] There are, for Dewey, two directions in which the search for security can be conducted. The first, which has been associated with the religious spirit and which has characterized most previous philosophies, is to accept things as they are by putting one's will, "even in sore affliction, on the side of the powers which dispense fortune." The second way of seeking security is "to invent arts and by their means turn the powers of nature to account; man constructs a fortress out of the very conditions and forces which threaten him." Human history is, according to Dewey, structured by the balance between "arts of acceptance" and "arts of control." The present age is the first one in which the arts of control have the living possibility of gaining ascendency in human society. Dewey's general program is that collective life be reoriented so that the arts of control will be used to their fullest extent and be turned toward achieving desirable ends.

Dewey is not a simple advocate of the scientific spirit, but a speculative philosopher whose thought joins the battle against traditional ontologies on their own ground. His critical purpose is to discredit the "elevation of knowledge above making and doing," and the "exaltation of pure intellect and its activity above practical affairs." He argues that the "traditional doctrine" that the intellect "may grasp universal Being," which is "fixed and immutable," is "fundamentally connected with the quest for a certainty which shall be absolute and unshakeable." The core of the quest for certainty is "man's distrust of himself," which has caused a desire "to get beyond and above himself." Traditional philosophy has responded to the idea that self-transcendence could be attained in "pure knowledge." Dewey, of course, does not believe that such pure knowledge of a fixed and immutable being is possible for finite thinkers. Thought, according to Dewey, is a function of social life, which appears in particular circumstances and has the function of preparing new responses to situations when the old ones have proven to be unsatisfactory. In Dewey's view, the quest for certainty cannot be satisfied because "practical activity," which is the only genuine activity, "involves change" and "deals with individualized and unique situations which are never exactly duplicable and about which, accordingly, no complete assurance is possible."[3] Practical activity evokes the "pathos of unfulfilled expectation" and the "tragedy of defeated purpose and ideals." However prudently executed action may be, humans never gain full control of its consequences. The outcome of any action includes the contribution of "alien and indifferent natural forces," and "unforeseeable conditions," which have a more "decisive voice" the more important the issue is.

Dewey's critique of the great tradition of ontology, then, is similar to the naturalistic criticisms of idealism mounted in nineteenth-century Europe by such thinkers as Karl Marx, Friedrich Nietzsche, and Sigmund Freud. The general strategy of naturalistic criticism is to counterpose a set of ideas that are declared to be false against a set of ideas that are claimed to be true, and then to explain the occurrence of the false ideas by the operation of a motive or psychological process which causes some thinkers to flee from the truth.[4] For example, Nietzsche's critique of *ressentiment* contrasts an ethic of self-sacrifice, which is held to deny life, with an ethic of life-affirmation, and accounts for the occurrence of the first ethic by appeal to a defective "will to power." The ethic of self-sacrifice, then, is the product of a disguised resentment against the vital strength of others. Dewey's critique of claims to knowledge of fixed and immutable being follows the naturalistic pattern by setting ideas of rational perfection against the categories of practical life, particularly the uniqueness of each situation and what the American existentialist David Swenson called "objective insecurity."[5] The appeal to ideas of rational perfection and especially to "the absolutely assured and permanent reality of the values with which practical activity is concerned" is grounded in self-distrust, which causes a desire for self-transcendence expressed as the quest for certainty. Thus, Dewey provides a naturalistic explanation, based in psychology, for traditional ontology.

Dewey's naturalistic account of the quest for certainty seems to imply a description of the human condition similar to that provided by the existentialists. Existence, for Dewey, is a series of unique situations in which the individual encounters objective insecurity about the future. Self-distrust is an outcome of the essential structure of the human condition and generates the will to self-transcendence. That will finds its object in rational ideas of perfection, particularly in the proposition that being is good, but such ideas falsify existence because they result from an evasion of the basic human condition. Authentic existence would involve full acceptance of the self-distrust involved in living and of the responsibility to decide in each situation with the awareness of risk and with no justifications. Self-transcendence in Dewey's sense, the desire "to get beyond and above oneself," would be opposed within one's own life and a project of self-overcoming would challenge it. Self-overcoming would be the very activity of resisting the desire for self-transcendence and of taking responsibility for one's own existence. Yet the project of self-overcoming would never be completed, because the quest for certainty and its existential grounds, the desire for self-transcendence and basic self-distrust, are constitutive of human existence. In Heidegger's sense, each one would keep "falling" from the heights of authentic existence.

The existential possibilities of Dewey's critique of traditional ontology can be deepened even further by noting that his overall thesis that human beings live in a world of hazards and are compelled to seek for security, and his subsidiary claim that objective insecurity generates self-distrust (subjective insecurity) may be radicalized to issue in James's panic fear of the "pit of insecurity" lying below the surface of life. Subjective insecurity is, from an existentialist viewpoint, the necessary correlate of objective insecurity. If the latter cannot be eliminated as a constitutive feature of human existence, then neither can the former. James described panic fear as a fear of his own existence, expressed specifically as a realization of his radical contingency. He eventually rationalized his panic fear by concealing it under ontological wonder-sickness and then under the will to believe. But he acknowledged the constitutive character of the quest for certainty, conceding, in fact, so much to it as to attempt a "justification of faith." The "arts of acceptance," which Dewey identifies as one of the two great ways of managing insecurity, are human responses to a subjective insecurity that generates an essential restlessness and dissatisfaction in human existence. When the restlessness becomes pointless and the dissatisfaction acute the individual is subject to *acedia*. It is at this moment of radical separation that the choice between self-transcendence and self-overcoming opens up. If the literature of existentialism be interpreted in these terms, Sören Kierkegaard and William James choose a pure act of self-transcendence, an act of faith, and Friedrich Nietzsche chooses the project of self-overcoming. Choice here, of course, is not meant in the sense of a detached calculator selecting among options, but in the sense of a commitment of the entire self to a life-plan.

Dewey does not develop the existentialist line of thought that is implicit in his critique of the rationalist philosophies based on the proposition that being is good. He brushes against existentialism by constructing categories of practicality based on objective insecurity, but his elimination of James's "theoretic" realm from his philosophy does not permit him to acknowledge the significance of the subjective insecurity to which he alludes. Dewey does not respond to James's challenge to affirm a pure empiricism, but covers up James's scandal by subordinating all forms of reasoning to practical reasoning. He is enabled to eliminate the "theoretic" realm, of which ontological wonder-sickness is the principle, by his acceptance of the common-sense assumption of an objective world. This "external world" is, as Santayana noted, an assumption of practicality, not a scientific hypothesis. Dewey's strategy, then, is to follow C. S. Peirce in promoting a "critical commonsensism."[6] Certain categories, the most important being that of an external world common to knowing actors, are taken for granted by philosophical reflection, the office of which is to evaluate the methods through which beliefs about that world are fixed. Philosophers can and should make the categories of practicality clear, but they should not question their status as the essential categories of human existence.

Dewey's evasion of the existentialist claims that are implicit in his critique of rationalism is made evident by the direction his argument takes after that critique is concluded. Having stated that "the verdict of our most enduring philosophic tradition" is that the "quest for complete certainty can be fulfilled in pure knowing alone," Dewey remarks that "it may be doubted whether if we were suddenly released from the burden of tradition, we should, on the basis of present experience take the disparaging view of practice and the exalted view of knowledge apart from action which tradition dictates." He notes that human beings have "learned to play with the sources of danger" and "even seek them out, weary of the routine of a too sheltered life." And then Dewey expresses the vision that, in his naturalism, substitutes for the experiences of the holiness of each moment and the communion of beings in being, which guided Josiah Royce and C. S. Peirce: "We have attained, at least subconsciously, a certain feeling of confidence; a feeling that control of the main conditions of fortune is to an appreciable degree passing into our own hands." Dewey speculates that "if contemporary western man were completely deprived of all the old beliefs about knowledge and actions he would assume, with a fair degree of confidence, that it lies within his power to achieve a reasonable degree of security in life."[7]

The gap in Dewey's thought between the critique of the quest for certainty and the promotion of the search for reasonable security is as deep as the abyss in James's thought between the "theoretic" realm and the practical realm, only Dewey does not seem to be aware of the dualism. When Dewey critiques rationalism, he identifies a quest of individual human beings for peace and completion in an inherently dangerous and hazardous world. When, however, he promotes reform he identifies a collective search of the species for "reasonable security." As did Royce, Peirce, and James, Dewey bases his life-commitment on deliverance to the community. But Dewey's community is not the ideal entity of his predecessors; it is the actual human species.

The deeper structure of Dewey's thought seems to be the same as that of James: it is fruitless, dangerous, and, therefore, immoral for a person to seek a merely individual security. Thus, human beings should devote themselves wholeheartedly to serving one another, to improving one another's lives. However, in contrast to James, Dewey evades his own insight that human beings quest for "complete certainty" and argues that, after all, they can be satisfied with "reasonable security." The new turn in his argument involves a historical appeal to cultural lag rather than a psychological and existential appeal to individual motivation. Having exhausted his critique of cognitive absolutes, Dewey shifts to his defense of reconstructive intelligence, claiming that the separation of theory and practice, "with its consequent substitution of cognitive quest for absolute assurance for practical endeavor to make the existence of good more secure in experience, has had the effect of distracting energy from a task whose performance would yield definite results." Dewey now explains the persistence of the split between theory and practice by "beliefs about values which have been widely accepted, which have prestige, which have become deeply impregnated with sentiment, and which authoritative institutions as well as the emotion and inertia of men are slow to surrender."[8] He claims that the difficulty "in the road is a practical one, a social one, connected with institutions and the methods and aims of education, not with science nor with value." Thus, Dewey transforms an initial situation in which individual human beings are constitutively insecure into a new situation in which the species progressively overcomes finite insecurities through intelligent application of the experimental method. This transformation is not performed overtly. Dewey does not bridge the gap between theory and practice that James opened up, but first acknowledges it and then ignores it. He is enabled to evade James's challenge to affirm a pure empiricism by cleaving to his vision of the control of the "main conditions of fortune" passing into human hands.

Dewey's primary concern and his major contribution to American philosophy was his effort to determine how control over nature could be used well. However, alongside his moral and political thought he pursued reflection on the "arts of acceptance." It was noted earlier that for the mystical visions of the initiators of American classical philosophy, the next generation of naturalists substituted resignation. Dewey's advocacy of resignation appears in his thought on religion. Although he proclaimed throughout his mature work a dynamic and progressive humanism, he did not altogether ignore the limitations encountered by finite individuals. *A Common Faith*, published in 1934, is Dewey's attempt to formulate an over-belief. In it he brings forward again the basic insecurity of human existence. He remarks that with the increase of "mechanisms of control" some "optimistic souls" have concluded that "the forces about us are on the whole essentially benign." Dewey charges that such optimism reflects "egoism rather than intelligent courage," though it is "the part of manliness to insist upon the capacity of mankind to strive to direct natural and social forces to humane ends." Thus, Dewey acknowledges that "when man, individually and collectively, has done his uttermost, conditions that at different times and places have given rise to the ideas of Fate and Fortune, of Chance and Providence, remain."[9] Nature, then, cannot be altogether rationalized and life cannot be affirmed for its own sake. There is a need for a faith to reconcile finite human beings to nature.

According to Dewey, who explicitly follows Friedrich Schleiermacher in this respect, the essence of religion is a sense of dependence on that which lies beyond the self and an accompanying feeling of humility.[10] Dewey makes the task of his natural religion the provision of an appropriate belief to which these feelings, which he judges to be universal, may be attached. He argues that the form taken by the sense of dependence should not be fear, because "fear never gave a stable perspective in the life of anyone." Adding that "our dependence is manifested in those relations to the environment that support our undertakings and aspirations as much as it is in the defeats inflicted upon us," and that it is "unreligious" to attribute "human achievement and purpose to man in isolation from the world of physical nature and his fellows," Dewey urges a "natural piety" that is neither a "fatalistic acquiescence in natural happenings" nor "a romantic idealization of the world." Dewey's definition of natural piety recalls James's sophisticated and paradoxical over-belief in which irreducible evil is necessary to provide incentive for strenuous commitment, and a tendency toward the good is necessary to stimulate transcendence of *acedia*. Dewey's expression of this paradox is "a just sense of nature as the whole of which we are parts" and the recognition that "we are parts that are marked by intelligence and purpose, having the capacity to strive by their aid to bring conditions into greater consonance with what is humanly desirable." Dewey concludes that the form of piety he recommends is "an inherent constituent of a just perspective in life."[11]

Dewey does not define what he means by a "just perspective" independently of his exposition of the "common faith," the devotion to "the doings and sufferings of the continuous human community in which we are a link." He holds that the "fact" that we are "all in the same boat traversing the same turbulent ocean" has potentially "infinite" religious significance, and that faith in humanity's improvement "has always been implicitly the common faith of mankind."[12] Thus, although Dewey's over-belief is similar in content to that of James, it is not grounded as an idea of practical reasoning, but appears to be rooted in the collective wisdom of the species and immanent to human nature. This interpretation is supported by Dewey's concluding remark in *A Common Faith* that it remains to make the implicit faith of humanity "explicit and militant." Dewey recurs to Peirce, not only for his starting point in "real and living doubt," but for his final life-commitment which affirms synechism. Dewey's synechism, however, has a moment of resignation in it because it has passed through James's critique of theodicy. Dewey does not affirm the communion of all beings in being, because the experienced cosmos is rife with alien and indifferent forces which cause insecurity and the very need for religion. He affirms, instead, the communion of all human beings in humanity and commends dedication to the "continuing life" of "this comprehensive community of beings" that "includes all the significant achievements of men in science and art and all the kindly offices of intercourse and communication." Acknowledgment of the "communal origin" of culture will indicate "its rightful communal use." The essence of Dewey's life-commitment is the absolutization of the "search for reasonable security." He did not return, in his religious thought, to the situation of the individual radically separated from the world by constitutive insecurity, but limited the ground for religion to objective insecurity. Thus, he evaded James's ontological wonder-sickness and was enabled to propound a humanistic piety. Implicit in Dewey's discussion of life-commitment is that the individual is saved from separation by the vision of species being.

Dewey's defense of humanity as the proper object of life-commitment is a direct continuation of Royce's vision of the community of minds in the absolute life, Peirce's regulative idea of the infinite community of inquirers, and James's fellowship of moral beings under divine obligation. For Dewey, who was born in 1859, four years after Royce and twenty-one after Peirce, moral vision did not spring from a retreat into the wilderness, but from reflection on the meaning of human history and on the activities that make up that history, such as science and politics. Philosophy, in Dewey's thought, is conducted in the city and has lost its special office of showing that the city and the wilderness are ruled by the same God. Dewey, however, did not abandon understanding the philosopher's vocation in terms of the image of wandering in a wilderness. In 1930 he wrote an autobiographical memoir, "From Absolutism to Experimentalism," in which he described his transition from his early attachment to Hegelian idealism to his mature naturalistic commitment. He concluded his memoir with a definition of the philosopher's task which is strikingly similar to that given by Royce in *The World and the Individual* with the single difference that for Dewey the wilderness is not set off from and placed in tension with the city. Having noted that "a chief task of those who call themselves philosophers is to help get rid of the useless lumber that blocks our highways of thought, and strive to make straight and open the paths that lead to the future," he wrote: "Forty years spent in wandering in a wilderness like that of the present is not a sad fate—unless one attempts to make himself believe that the wilderness is after all itself the promised land."[13] Dewey here touches the most profound level of his thought, indicating that in the twentieth century the city itself may be depicted as a wilderness that should be redeemed by the constructive efforts of human beings. By teaching that the present age is a wilderness Dewey may be judged to have made an advance on James, an advance similar to that achieved by Martin Luther when he preached that the separation of monastery and world should be abolished.

The experience of panic fear, which overcame James when he was thrown into the wilderness of radical separation, left lasting effects of American thought. James's willful abandonment of "theoretic" contemplation and his exploration of practical reasoning as a means to promote the zest for life became in Dewey's thought the declaration that there is no human viewpoint other than practicality. James responded to the absence of the God of the wilderness, to the death of God, by trying to fashion a more tolerant and generous God of the city who would allow for the florescence of individuality, which the God of the wilderness had once protected. James's God was so limited as to be constrained by the empiricist ethic of inner tolerance. Dewey, in contrast, held that the God implicit in human history is the God of the city, humanity itself, interpreted as a continuous community spanning the generations and redeeming itself. Human beings, in Dewey's vision, no longer had any means of separating themselves from the city, which might itself take on the character of wilderness. Any attempt to do so was "self-contradictory" and explicable through a depth psychology that derived the desire for self-transcendence from self-distrust. Radical separation was, for Dewey, an illusion in a different way than it was for Royce and Peirce. In the idealistic phase of American classical philosophy apparent separation was overcome through a reasoned vision of continuity. The path to community ran through the wilderness and moral education was backed by ontological reflection. James's critique of ontological wonder-sickness barricaded the path into the wilderness of personal and agonized doubting, and left the project of moral education, urging people to be loyal to one another, without support. Dewey's humanism was an attempt to provide a new support for moral education, but it failed because it was not, by virtue of Dewey's clear-sightedness, based on the confident assertion that being is good. Dewey's appeal to depth psychology as a means of discrediting claims to radical separation indicates his own faltering confidence. Royce and Peirce had redeemed separation through vision; Dewey attempted to undermine it through a critique of false consciousness.

The content of Dewey's program of moral education is a critique of party spirit and as such it falls squarely within the tradition of American classical philosophy. Dewey tied his religious thought directly to his moral appeal, urging that his "common faith" was not "confined to sect, class, or race." In *The Quest for Certainty* he concludes his discussion of religion with a critique of pride, which is the evil lying at the root of the false separation of the self from others. Dewey remarks that one of "the deepest of moral traditions is that which identifies the source of moral evil, as distinct from retrievable error, with pride, and which identifies pride with isolation." He says that pride assumes many forms and appears among those who "profess the most complete dependence." Dewey's greatest concern is directed at "the pride of the zealously devout," which he calls "the most dangerous form of pride" because it "generates an exclusive institutionalism" and fills those who have it with the feeling that they are "special organs of the divine."[14] Dewey's primary objection to zealous pride is that it denies "interaction and interdependence" by confining "to special channels the power of those who profess special connection with the ideal and spiritual." The zealously devout have a confidence that the naturalists lack; they believe that their relation to the divine gives them "authority over others."

Dewey introduces into his discussion of pride at the conclusion of *The Quest for Certainty* a moral argument against the separation of theory and practice that counterbalances his depth-psychological analysis at the beginning of the work. He claims that zealous pride that seeks a "spiritual monopoly" condemns "other modes of human association to an inferior position and role" and "breeds irresponsibility" in these other modes of association. He believes that the creation of irresponsibility is "perhaps the most serious of the many products of that dualism between nature and spirit in which isolation of the actual and the possible eventuates."[15] The "most corroding form of spiritual pride and isolation," the separation of the spiritual from the natural, and the elevation of a realm of spirit over a realm of nature, has made human beings believe that activities devoted to preserving and improving the material conditions of life are inferior to activities of the mind, and, therefore, that the material life need not be subjected to the highest moral standards. Here Dewey inverts Karl Marx's argument that the separation of brain from muscle is a result of the organization of production, and traces the pattern of economic organization to a cultural dualism. Dewey, then, begins *The Quest for Certainty* as a depth psychologist and ends it as a secular or cultural theologian warning against pride and urging humility.

Dewey's critique of pride recalls Peirce's criticism of the "method of authority," the collectivized variant of "tenacity," as a way of fixing belief. Dewey's addition to Peirce's claim that authority, in the long run, produces maladaptation to reality is that zealous pride fosters disrespect for all but the activities deemed worthy by the authority. The separation of a spiritual elite from the rest of the community is "the source of the deepest and most injurious of all enmities." Dewey's gift to the community is his critique of philosophical and theological elitism. He attempts to make good on Royce's claim that the philosopher is not superior to other human beings by reducing the task of philosophy to that of "liaison officer between the conclusions of science and the modes of social and personal action through which attainable possibilities are projected and striven for." Yet he cannot forsake the office of American classical philosophy to stimulate the achievement of a moral community through teaching a "conception of the frame of things." His vocation culminates in arousing the community to "a sense of common participation in the inevitable uncertainties of existence." He believes that this sense of continuity with others would be "coeval with a sense of common effort and shared destiny." Dewey's promise is that a sense of dependence, purified of dogma, would encourage cooperative and voluntary experimentation by the members of the ongoing historical community to achieve greater security for "excellence of all kinds" in "experienced existence."[16] Dewey does not provide a list of "excellencies" ranged in an immutable hierarchy. Tables of value are, for him, provisional and mutable. His absolute is religious in the broad sense of that term; it is a proper spirit of deliverance to community, a generous spirit that overcomes zealous pride.

The hope that informed much of Dewey's work was that if philosophers, and others who were privileged enough to have developed intellects, renounced their pride and devoted themselves to social reconstruction through democratic methods, the vision of a self-controlling community would be realized. Dewey feared that the isolation of religious and moral reflection from material life would produce an industrial machine that might destroy the natural community. In his polemical work, *Liberalism and Social Action*, published in 1935, Dewey carried his critique of separation into political advocacy, arguing that both classical liberalism and revolutionary Marxism isolated human beings from one another in competitive relations.[17] Neither one of these doctrines, according to Dewey, understood that the modern spirit is that of free inquiry, Peirce's "scientific spirit." Thus, both classical liberalism and revolutionary Marxism were attempts to adjust to the changes wrought by science and technology through the imposition of rigid methods of social action such as particularistic competition and class conflict. Yet, according to Dewey, science is informed by cooperation, which allows it to develop ever more effective means of material transformation. Were the scientific spirit of cooperation to be extended to social reconstruction, the dangers of the industrial machine to the natural community would be at least reduced and, perhaps, overcome. Taking Dewey's thought as a whole, the devotion to experimental social reconstruction depended on a spiritual transformation that would abolish the illusory split of theory from practice and would ground both theory and practice in the "sense of common participation in the inevitable uncertainties of existence."

Dewey's appeal to commitment to the community despite the constitutive imperfection of practical life marks an advance over the life-philosophies of Royce, Peirce, and James. All three of Dewey's predecessors believed that it was necessary to stimulate commitment by providing ideas of perfection, whether they were constitutive of existence (Royce), regulative over it (Peirce), or postulated by the will as its dynamizing principle (James). Dewey substituted for ideas of perfection an idea of shared imperfection. The weakness of his view, from an existential standpoint, however, is that he mediated commitment to others through emotion. Here he fell back from James's insight that the crown of empiricism is a spirit of inward tolerance. The spirit of inward tolerance demands an act of will that works in the opposite direction to the will to believe and that tempers enthusiasm with an inner reserve or "inner check." Inner tolerance is voluntary self-limitation, which is the essence of moral freedom because it provides a noncompulsive restriction on communal activity. Dewey, whose naturalism required him to reject the radical separation of the self from the world implied by voluntarism, resorted to a feeling in order to regulate collective action. Thus, he replaced the idealist's reliance upon reasoned vision with reliance upon a unifying emotion. Both vision and emotion, however, are merely items that appear within experience alongside others. They do not call experience itself into question, as do ontological wonder-sickness and its existential root, panic fear. Only when experience is so called into question does the deciding self emerge to make a decision for or against life. Agonized doubting is intrinsically related to inner tolerance through the act of self-control involved in both. By failing to raise the question of being radically, Dewey closed the circle opened by Peirce's infinite with resignation.

6

George Santayana

George Santayana was the only member of the group of American classical philosophers to have placed himself outside the American cultural tradition. Although he was educated in philosophy at Harvard University and taught there for more than twenty years, Santayana remarked in the preface to his commentary on American thought, *Character and Opinion in the United States*, that he was not an American, "except by long association," and that he could only try to understand the heart of the nation "as a family friend may who has a different temperament."[1] The great difference in Santayana's temperament from those of the other American classical philosophers is illustrated by his observation in *Reason in Common Sense* that "the age of controversy is past; that of interpretation has succeeded."[2]

Santayana did not believe that his task was to construct ideals but only to interpret them, "confronting them with one another and with the conditions which, for the most part, they alike ignore." He did not initiate his speculations with a moment of doubt or with any withdrawal into the wilderness. He was a philosopher of the city and was suspicious of any claims that truth could be discovered in the wilderness of pure experience or of pure reflection. In the preface to his treatise on methodical doubting, *Scepticism and Animal Faith*, Santayana wrote: "I stand in philosophy exactly where I stand in daily life; I should not be honest otherwise. I accept the same miscellaneous witnesses, bow to the same obvious facts, make conjectures no less instinctively, and admit the same encircling ignorance." He trusted and made the ground of his philosophic thought "a certain shrewd orthodoxy which the sentiment and practice of laymen maintain everywhere." Santayana's goal was to be honest about what he believed, not to be pretentious; never to make any claims that he was not willing to live by, but always to try to live by what he could not help but believe. He claimed that his endeavor was "to think straight in such terms as are offered to me, to clear my mind of cant and free it from the cramp of artificial traditions; but I do not ask any one to think in my terms if he prefers others."[3] Santayana issued invitations instead of promulgating edicts. He had an acute awareness of the limits of the philosopher's influence on the conduct of everyday life and sought to bring speculative thought closer to the principles of that conduct, as he believed Plato and Socrates had done.

Santayana's naturalism was a response to what he judged to be the cant and artificiality of the modern philosophic tradition, especially as evinced in German idealism, the spirit of which he believed was the dominant influence in American philosophy. Idealism, according to Santayana, was an expression of egotism because it assigned the constitution of experience to the self rather than to nature, which tolerated and, perhaps, encouraged in some circumstances the emergence and persistence of selves. At the core of Santayana's "natural philosophy" is the principle that "the origin of beliefs and ideas, as of all events, is natural." By natural he meant "material," in the sense of a substance which could generate all of the different kinds of events that make up experience. Santayana did not claim to have an intuition of the matter that he postulated; it was one of the categories he devised for clarifying the "shrewd orthodoxy" maintained by laymen, a kind of universal common sense that he held was immanent to civilized life. Santayana claimed that the "warrant" for his naturalism was "public experience": "My philosophy is justified, and has been justified in all ages and countries, by the facts before every man's eyes; and no great wit is requisite to discover it, only (what is rarer than wit) candour and courage."[4] Santayana judged nineteenth-century idealism wanting because it lacked the candor to admit that its transcendental reflections were play-acting and the courage to take the consequences of the demythologization of religion. He believed that the major consequence of Nietzsche's "death of

God" decree for life-philosophy was the need, in civilization, for a sturdy and classical materialism based on acceptance of personal finitude and on affirmation of the goods that appear in the flux of experience. Although he claimed not to ask his readers to think in his terms if they preferred others, Santayana spent his life as a thinker pursuing the vocation of moral philosopher, commending his materialism to others.

Santayana's thought acknowledges both lived doubt and methodical doubt, but it does not acknowledge or comprehend wondering doubt or its root, panic fear. Santayana criticizes William James's thought in *Character and Opinion in the United States*, published in 1920, where he praises James for his early psychological inquiries, but criticizes his later empiricism. According to Santayana, James "professed to begin his study on the assumptions of common sense, that there is a material world which the animals that live in it are able to perceive and to think about." However, Santayana notes, had James pursued this naturalistic path he would have had "to admit that nature was automatic and mind simply cognitive, conclusions from which every instinct in him recoiled." Thus, James was "insensibly" carried away from any reliance upon the category of matter and toward the position that "flux itself" was "the fundamental existence": "The *sense* of bounding over the waves, the *sense* of being on an adventurous voyage, was the living fact; the rest was dead reckoning."[5]

Santayana held that practical experience refers beyond itself to a world of external things and that when empiricism "ceases to value experience as a means of discoverng external things" it can "give up its ancient prejudice in favor of sense as against imagination, for imagination and thought are immediate experiences as much as sensation is: they are therefore, for absolute empiricism, no less actual ingredients of reality."[6] For Santayana, an "absolute empiricism" such as James proposed would lead to a loss of the distinctions between dream and reality, and wish and circumstance, upon which common sense is based. For common sense, there must be a realm of fact to which interpretations are relative. This principle of common sense is, for Santayana, "instinctive"; it is integral to "animal faith." The denial of the principle shows either confusion or malice, because, for Santayana, it is malicious to deny the shrewd orthodoxy of the race, which, if one were honest with oneself, candid and courageous enough, one would confess to believing. Common sense, of course, is the wisdom of the city, the precipitate of "public experience." It is the social version of the world, which aids the everyday survival of groups. Santayana did not believe that there was any possible wisdom to be found beyond the confines of this "instinctive" and socially funded set of interpretations. Thus, he did not acknowledge even the possibility that radical separation, which issued in ontological wonder-sickness or, more profoundly, in panic fear might provide access to truths about existence.

James's empiricism, as was shown in the fourth chapter of this work, is not based on an insensible movement from materialistic psychology to "absolute empiricism," but on the insight that appearance is, when contrasted with the possibility of nothingness, self-sustaining. James stated in "The Sentiment of Rationality" that, at least for him, the affirmation of empiricism was grounded in ontological wonder. He returned, throughout his work, to the idea that experience as a whole stands out against the backdrop of nothingness. In his *Pragmatism*, published in 1907, he wrote that for "pluralistic pragmatism," truth "grows up inside of all the finite experiences," which "lean on each other, but the whole of them, if such a whole there be, leans on nothing." He continued, in terms that are close to those of Martin Heidegger, that "all 'homes' are in finite experience; finite experience as such is homeless: . . . Nothing outside of the flux secures the issue of it. It can hope salvation only from its own intrinsic promises and potencies."[7] James, then, did not understand his empiricism to be actuated by recoil from the thesis that nature is automatic and mind simply cognitive, but by the experience of wondering about why there are beings rather than not. He interpreted his empiricism as the issue of theoretic reason and not as a postulate of practical reasoning, as Santayana seems to claim that it is. From the viewpoint of practical reasoning, James chose an idealistic over-belief because he thought that such a "conception of the frame of things" would be the most effective stimulus to the will to live and to moral conduct. He would, perhaps, have considered Santayana's materialism to have counseled too much passivity, but he would have welcomed it as another "frame of things" that might allow some people to summon the will to live and to add whatever contribution they could make to the community. It is clear, however, that James would not have given any more standing to Santayana's naturalism than that of another over-belief that functioned in the realm of practical reasoning. He would not have allowed any wisdom about how to live to be judged as a universal orthodoxy or a set of beliefs instinctive to the race.

Santayana's resort to common sense as a ground for his life-philosophy is similar to Dewey's appeal to a common faith, which is supposed to be immanent to humanity. In both cases some collective wisdom about how to live and what to live for is made to stand for the discredited visions of an earlier idealism. Just as Dewey may be usefully considered as a transposer of Peirce's regulative idealism into the naturalistic key, so Santayana's thought may be understood as a transposition of Royce's absolute idealism into materialism. Viewed as an intelligible history, American classical philosophy begins with absolute idealism, which is rooted in the sanctification of each moment, moves to a regulative idealism in which reality and existence are separated, passes through the needle's eye of nothingness and ontological wonder, and then loops back to metaphysics, but now naturalistic and materialistic. For this intelligible history, Santayana's is the last moment of American classical philosophy because it carries out the inversion of absolute idealism into materialism, which Santayana claims is a philosophy of old age and ripened life.

Santayana did not fully understand James's radical empiricism because he did not acknowledge its origins in wondering doubt, and even more deeply in the agonized doubt of panic fear. Santayana did comprehend, thoroughly and precisely, Royce's method of transcendental doubting, which is the terminus of Cartesian feigned doubt. One of the great paradoxes of Santayana's thought is that although he claimed repeatedly to base his philosophy upon the principles of common sense, the method that he discussed and critiqued in his inquiries was transcendental. In *Character and Opinion in the United States* Santayana discusses Royce's method and provides a capsule statement of his own position. Santayana begins by noting that Royce's "technical method" is "pure transcendentalism." This method, according to Santayana, is "an attitude or a point of view rather than a system," and its "Absolute is thinking 'as such,' wherever thought may exert itself." Transcendentalism, which is the critique of knowledge in terms of what is given in thought with certainty, excludes knowledge of anything but actual thinking. Excluded entities, thus, in-

clude finite selves, relations among thinkers, any infinite self, separate instances of thought, and material objects: "*Any* system of
existences, *any* truth or matter of fact waiting to be recognised,
contradicts the transcendental insight and stultifies it."[8] According to Santayana, the result of applying the method of transcendental doubting consistently and thoroughly is "solipsism of the
present moment." He adds, speaking directly to Royce's idealism,
that the "all-inclusive mind is my mind as I think, mind in its living
function, and beyond that philosophy cannot go."

Following his characteristic criticism of all idealists, Santayana
argues that Royce, though he often employed the transcendental
method, "could not help believing that constructive fancy not only
feigns individuals and instances of thought, but is actually seated
in them." However, the transcendental method does not result in
any certainty but the certainty of the actual thought; all discourse
about individuals and instances of thought is only that: discourse
in a present moment. The references to a "beyond," which Royce
believed were inherent within each moment of thought, are merely thoughts of a reference to a beyond. For Santayana, there is no
escape from the present moment when it is made the terminus of
transcendental reflection. The escape from solipsism is living and
all of the assumptions inherent in it, which philosophy should
clarify and which prove to be consistent with common sense. Santayana's master principle of transcendental criticism is that nothing given exists; what is given in thought is an appearance, an essence, which is exactly what it is and needs no supplementation.
Yet transcendentalists are unwilling or unable to let the present
moment be. They strive to make it yield knowledge of objective reality, particularly knowledge that is in harmony with their deepest
wishes, such as personal immortality or the endurance of what
they hold to be good. Transcendentalists, according to Santayana,
are enabled to engage in wish fulfillment of this sort only because
they have not been candid and courageous enough in applying
their method. They do not carry the method through to its final
conclusion, but stop short, before the ending, at some supposed
irreducible term, such as Descartes's thinking substance. In
Royce's case, the Absolute, interpreted as "an actual synthetic universal mind," and the existence of "many collateral human minds,
in temporal existential relations to one another" were superadded
to the solipsism of the present moment. Royce was thereby en-

abled to make his philosophy a vehicle for his wishes that appeared to be relevant to the problems of everyday life; but only at the cost of severe inconsistency in his thought.

Santayana comments that if Royce had thought through the relation between his transcendentalism and his "social realism" he would have had to claim that knowledge was "only faith leaping across the chasm of coexistence and guessing the presence and nature of what surrounds us by some hint of material influence or brotherly affinity." However, Santayana adds, both "the credulity and the finality which such naturalism implies were offensive to Royce, and contrary to his sceptical and mystical instincts."[9] For Santayana, Royce had committed the "pathetic fallacy" of projecting his wishes into reality rather than keeping firm the distinction between wish and reality. Existence, according to Santayana, must be commodious enough to generate and to tolerate all of the appearances that we intuit, and it is a sign of cowardice and insecurity for a thinker to pretend that reality can be known to be better than is indicated by what appears to us. The misapplication of their method by the transcendentalists was not, then, merely a cognitive error, but was more deeply rooted in moral failing. Santayana noted in *Reason in Common Sense* that "to misrepresent the conditions and consequences of action is no merely speculative error; it involves a false emphasis in character and an artificial balance and co-ordination among human pursuits."[10] Santayana strove not to make things seem to be better than they really were and constructed his naturalism so that the "conditions and consequences of action" would be fairly represented. However, he may be critiqued for not having been a severe enough critic. The "shrewd orthodoxy" upon which he relied for his over-belief is sober and well adapted to the finite concerns of practical life, but it does not drink of life fully and discover that beneath and around its springs is nothing.

Late in his life, in a 1948 letter to Arthur A. Cohen, Santayana expressed some of his judgments on Kierkegaard's thought and on twentieth-century existentialism. With regard to *Angst*, the dread experienced before James's "pit of insecurity," Santayana queried: "Is not such Angst a disease, an emotion produced by Protestant theology after faith in that theology has disappeared?" With respect to nothingness, the pit or abyss itself, Santayana states that he has read "more or less of Heidegger, and liked his analysis of 'pure' ideas, such as Nothing or Death." However, Santayana does not grasp the ontological dimension of Heideggerian no-thing, claiming that Heidegger considers Nothing and Death to be vacant notions: "He sees perfectly that the intrinsic vacancy of these notions lends them the function of repeating or framing-in positive objects, as death, by terminating a life, makes a biographical unit and moral finality of it."[11] Rather, indeed, than nothingness, the matrix in which Santayana lodges the strip of conscious and personal experience is "matter," which though it has no essential determination, is the positive ground of a world of transitive relations.

That Santayana did not understand the significance of nothingness for Heidegger and by implication for James is evidenced in his critique of Kierkegaard when he responds to the query: "And what is this self that feels the *Angst* and leaps heroically for salvation into the Unknown?" He remarks that if it is the "transcendental Self" then "it could feel no anxiety because it can be only transcendental," a pure activity of intuiting essences. If, in contrast, "this self is the concrete human psyche or person we know perfectly what its circumstances are and what it needs to be anxious about: . . . There may be wise or foolish decisions made by it, but no leap into the unknown."[12] By splitting "self" or "spirit" from "psyche," Santayana breaks apart the unity of Heideggerian "being-in-the-world" that makes dread and concern over one's finitude intelligible. In Santayana's scheme, spirit receives the portion of eternity and psyche of time. For Heidegger and also for James there is no such clear division between what belongs to God and what is due to Caesar. Indeed, for both of them commitment involves the total deliverance of the person, just because it is a "leap into the unknown."

Santayana did not employ the transcendental method of doubting in order to gain a fresh start for philosophy, the way Descartes and Royce, for example, had done. His major work in philosophical method, *Scepticism and Animal Faith*, published in 1923, begins with the observation that "a philosopher is compelled to follow the maxim of epic poets and to plunge *in medias res*." The philosophical vocation of providing an interpretation of a rational life, not a rational interpretation of life, is pursued by those who have an interest in and talent for it. The vocation is not generated by learning a method or by attempting seriously to doubt what one does not actually doubt. Santayana, then, is much more an interpreter of the transcendental method than a serious practitioner of it for philosophical purposes of discovering truth. The transcendental method, of which *Scepticism and Animal Faith* is an evaluation, is applicable to one of the three "different series or orders" into which human beliefs and ideas may be "arranged systematically." The "order of evidence" arises when the question is raised of what one is most certain, and what one believes only on hearsay or by suggestion, "which might be suspended or reversed." Santayana concludes that the transcendental method is correctly applied in the order of evidence and that its conclusion is: "I have absolute assurance of nothing save of the character of some given essence; the rest is arbitrary belief or interpretation added by my animal impulse." However, the order of evidence is but one of the ways in which beliefs and ideas may be arranged systematically. The "order of genesis" is an arrangement of beliefs according to origins, which are material. All origins, for Santayana, "lie in the realm of matter, even when the being that is so generated is immaterial, because this creation or intrusion of the immaterial follows on material occasions and at the promptings of circumstance."[13] The order of evidence is composed of intransitive essences, including the essence of transition. It is the "bed-rock of perfect certitude," which "turns out to be in the regions of the rarest ether." The order of genesis is made up of the actual processes of nature, which are not directly observable, but which may be represented symbolically by scientific theories. Thus, what is given does not exist and, by contraposition, what exists is not given.

Santayana also discusses a third order, the "order of discovery, in which beliefs and ideas are surveyed in the series in which "they come to be discriminated." The order of discovery places goods and evils first and is, therefore, "essentially romantic: . . . Will or moral bias is actually the background on which images of objects are gradually deciphered by an awakening intellect; they all appear initially loaded with moral values and assigned to rival camps and quarters in the field of action."[14] The order of discovery is the realm of human importance, the crown of which is the "life of reason," in which the most complete possible range of goods is reflexively harmonized and enacted. Short of the life of reason are the more militant and exclusivist systems of values that achieve limited harmonies by suppressing interests incompatible with the overriding concerns. The order of discovery is the home of "literary psychology," the imaginative construction of systems of human meaning and purpose. As opposed to "behavioral psychology," which is a record of fact and is rooted in the order of genesis, literary psychology is a personal history of the heart. No study is closer to human interest than literary psychology, but "none is more hopelessly the sport of apperception and of dramatic bias in the telling." The order of genesis and the sciences that express its configuration are the great teachers of limitation, and speak with the "authority of things" behind them. The order of evidence is the focus of a nearly inhuman and detached contemplation of essences, which is fit only for certain minds that have been freed from intense vital drives and have, thus, achieved a "spiritual freedom." Human beings are most at home in the order of discovery, where their desires and fears overshadow fact and form.

Santayana's complaint against romantic metaphysicians, who claimed to use the transcendental method, is that they confused the order of evidence and the order of discovery by purporting to adduce evidence for the existential fulfillment of personal desires. If the crown of the order of discovery is the life of reason, then its thorn is the pathetic fallacy, the propensity to believe that one's wishes are destined to be fulfilled existentially. Santayana found that the "realm of essence," which is opened up by the transcendental method, was the source of peaceful joy just because it is a realm of pure possibility and not a field for self-overcoming in pursuit of a particular idea of perfection. The transcendental method disclosed, for Santayana, an aesthetic dimension, a domain for the free play of disinterested spirit that is spoiled by any intrusion of the vital and selective will. Here Santayana falls within the tradition of classical vitalism, initiated by Schopenhauer, in which the will to live is interpreted as an inherently flawed will, which it is best to overcome by ascetic discipline. Even further back, the inclination to disinterested contemplation recalls Spinoza and Epicurus, two of Santayana's acknowledged masters. But contemplation of essence wars against the life of reason as well as against the militant imposition of wish on the world. Santayana's thought is divided by the impulses to moral education, expressed in his defense of common sense and of the life of reason, and to disinterested contemplation, expressed in his attempt to vindicate the radical essentiality of the immediate datum. The two sides of his thought are united negatively by his critique of egotism and its cognitive form, the pathetic fallacy.

By "scepticism" Santayana means the use of the transcendental method and by "animal faith" he means the instinctual presuppositions that form practical life. Animal faith is not a commitment that succeeds in time a withdrawal into the wilderness. Rather it is "an expression of hunger, pursuit shock, or fear," which is "directed upon *things;* that is, it assumes the existence of alien self-developing beings, independent of knowledge, but capable of being affected by action." Animal faith is an automatic positing of substances and an indication of their locus in a "field of action of which the animal occupies the centre." For the individuated life, existence is a career of discriminating between "dominations," which are unfavorable to its sustenance, and "powers," which are beneficent to it. The good life, from the viewpoint of the organism, is the elimination or overcoming of dominations, and the release and heightening of powers. The rational life, which may be possible for some thinking organisms, if circumstances are propitious, is a reflexive review of the objects of desire and the means to their achievement, and a course of action in accordance with the results of intelligent thought. However, the line that leads from animal faith to the life of reason is paralleled by another one that is anchored in the order of evidence, once that order has been purified. Santayana introduces the idea of "spirit" to refer to "the pure light or actuality of thought, common to all intuitions, in which essences are bathed if they are given." Unlike animal faith in which sharp distinctions are made between good and evil, and friend and foe, spirit is "inherently addressed to everything impartially, and is always, in its own principle, ready to be omniscient and just." Indeed, Santayana inverts Royce's idea of wilderness and comments that a mind "free from all tormenting anxiety about its own fortunes or existence, finds in the wilderness of essence a very sweet and marvellous solitude." The line that originates in the solipsism of the present moment, leads to an "ideal of the spirit, not only to extend its view over all time and all existence, but to exchange its accidental viewpoint for every other, and adopt every insight and every interest: an effort which, by a curious irony, might end in abolishing all interests and all views."[15] Thus, in Santayana's thought the exclusivity of animal faith wars against the inclusivity of spirit. Santayana does not propound a single life-commitment, but offers two life-possibilities.

The opposition between the "vital liberty," which grows out of animal faith, and the "spiritual freedom," which fulfills skepticism, is placed in context by recalling Royce's discussion of the attitudes of the will in his *The Problem of Christianity*. In that work Royce analyzed three attitudes, the first of which was affirmation of the will to live, or primal self-assertion; the second of which was denial of the will to live, or resignation; and the third of which was loyalty, or "a positive devotion of the Self to its cause." What is missing in Santayana's materialistic inversion of Royce's absolute idealism is a cause or, for that matter, any mediation between Schopenhauer's two poles of primal self-assertion and resignation. In Santayana's thought American classical philosophy comes full circle, except that an absolute materialism has been substituted for absolute idealism. The new materialism breaks the pattern of American life-philosophy by leaving its poles unmediated by an ideal of commitment to the community. The life of reason is, indeed, a moral ideal, but it is one among many and is only achieved when material conditions are propitious. It is not absolute and is under the judgment of spiritual freedom, which has equal ontological standing to it. There is no striving in Santayana's life-philosophy and no call for deliverance to the common task. He belongs, through the terms of his discourse, to the line of American classical philosophers, but he removed the puritan nerve from that tradition.

In a technical sense, the most significant alteration that Santayana made in Royce's general pattern of thought was to split the present moment from ongoing practical life, and to interpret the former as radically intransitive and the latter as radically transitive. From the standpoint of spirit, as Santayana interpreted it, the present moment did not have to be consecrated, but was already holy, in the sense of being whole. The present datum had only to be appreciated; it was not a steppingstone to anything greater than itself or an indication of a superior mental reality analogous to it in structure. From the standpoint of the living psyche, in contrast, there was no present moment at all, but a perpetual movement to actualize potentials by skirting or overcoming dominations, and by enhancing powers. The two poles of experience, passive transcendence over the world and active transcendence into it, were sharply severed from one another by Santayana. One might cultivate worldly success, with more or less reflection and comprehension, or one might nurture the intellectual love of God, but not both. Santayana had no mystical vision of an all-encompassing and completed eternal present to provide him with the confidence to act. In the place of such a vision he conceived of a "realm of truth," consisting of all of the essences that had ever been exemplified in the material flux. Santayana's realm of truth had no purposive integrity to it, either immanent or transcendent, and was a kind of absurd absolute, incomplete and imperfectly coherent. The implication of the realm of truth for life-philosophy was that there could be meanings actualized within an individuated life, but there could be no meaning of life itself. Life was a phase of the greater flux and the supreme wisdom was to be grateful for living and for having the opportunity, however brief, to be aware.

Santayana's dualism splits theory and practice, but not in the same way as William James did in "The Sentiment of Rationality." For Santayana, the two life-possibilities are both positive. Animal faith and its outgrowth of vital liberty are grounded in the positivity of essential intuition. There is, in Santayana's thought, no hint that appearance itself might be suspended in nothingness. Santayana's life-philosophy is an uneasy mixture of classical vitalism and transcendentalism, the first providing the dynamic or Dionysian element of the flux and the second providing the static or Apollonian element of form. Flux is as close as Santayana comes to naming the mystery of being. His theoretic realm of essential intuition does not contain the abyss, but is a retreat from the cares of everyday life, where it is possible to experience a disinterested peace: the domain of spiritual freedom is a kind of Epicurean garden of the mind. Santayana noted in the preface to *Reason in Common Sense* that "from childhood up I had lived in imagination, being fond of religion and poetry, and driven by circumstances to lead my inner life alone."[16] He went on to say that transcendental philosophy encouraged his "subjective habit," but that he never made subjectivity more than "a method, a habit of poetic sympathy with the dreaming mind, whatever it might dream." For Santayana it was essential that dream be sharply demarcated from reality, if only so that he could safely and sanely dream. That which is given does not exist, but it *is*. Santayana fashioned a realm of essence so that he could dream well and long.

Santayana made an effort to synthesize the poles of his life and thought by working out a cultural reconciliation of wish and fact through the concept of philosophical poetry. In his *Three Philosophical Poets,* published in 1910, the movement of Santayana's thought follows a dialectical pattern that evinces Hegelian tracings. The naive and initial moment of human spirit is confusion of dream and reality, of inner and outer. The second moment is one that betrays unhappy consciousness in its formal sense, an irreconcilable duality, a failure of the spirit to think the rational necessity of its ideal completion. Ideal and real are put into two different realms, the inner life is severed from the outer. In his rebellion against idealism Santayana refuses to complete the dialectic in a Hegelian fashion, but he does not stop at the stage of unhappy consciousness. The third stage of the movement of Santayana's thought belongs, as does the first, to our visions of perfection, but they are visions chastened by the critical intellect, aware of the limitations of imagination, and informed by the scientific view of nature. The highest stage of the spirit is what Santayana calls philosophical poetry, of which the works of Lucretius, Dante, and Goethe are among the best representatives. The philosophical poet extracts the essence from religion, relieving it of the pathetic fallacy, turning it into art, and giving it attraction to reason by fusing imagination with natural piety. The philosophical poet creates a synthesis of dream and reality, but one that transmutes reality into dream and not, as Hegel wished, one that transmutes dream into reality. The vision of a philosophical poet is both personal and civilized, expressing a specific scale of values, but doing so with the accent on appreciation and not on moral direction. Comparing the act of philosophical poetry to a "supreme dramatic crisis," in which "all our life seems to be focused in the present, and used in colouring our consciousness and shaping our decisions," Santayana remarks that "for each philosophical poet the whole world of man is gathered together; and he is never so much of a poet as when, in a single cry, he summons all that has affinity to him in the universe, and salutes his ultimate destiny."[17] Santayana concludes that philosophical poetry is the fulfillment of life because "it is the acme of life to understand life."

Santayana wrote *Three Philosophical Poets* before World War I and while he was still at Harvard University. In his later work cultural synthesis and the substitution of poetry for natural theology declined in their importance for his thought and greater emphasis on spiritual freedom took their place. However, even in the defense of philosophical poetry Santayana's inversion of Royce's idealism is clear. The entire tradition of American classical philosophy, of which Royce is the paradigmatic figure, was, until Santayana's critique, based on the primacy of moral commitment over any other human possibility. The raison d'être for speculative thought was, for Royce, Peirce, James, and Dewey, the search for a ground on which to undertake the project of moral education. Thought was to be placed in the service of moral development, perhaps especially for the rationalistic Royce who believed that the human vocation was to learn the absolute will by participating strenuously in the work of the great community.

Santayana overturned the table of values set up by the American puritan philosophers and replaced it with another one in which the supreme principle was that "the acme of life is to understand life." The difference between his "temperament" and those of the other American classical philosophers was expressed by his giving the last word to contemplation while they gave it to action. According to Santayana the "true philosopher" is a solitary figure whose "mission" is "to pilot himself, or at most a few voluntary companions, who may find themselves in the same boat." Philosophers should try to discover "if there is some deep and settled need in the heart of man, to give direction to his efforts." Such a pursuit, which is meditative, is, for Santayana, nearly impossible to carry out in America. In America "you must wave, you must cheer, you must push with the irresistible crowd; otherwise you will feel like a traitor, a soulless outcaste, a deserted ship high and dry on the shore."[18] Here Santayana presents his own version of the agony of the American philosopher. Dewey, for example, was not content to pilot a small boat with a few voluntary companions, but dedicated himself to announcing that all of us are in the same boat and that we should all row together. From Santayana's viewpoint, Dewey and the other American classical philosophers were so concerned that we should all join in the rowing that they forgot about piloting altogether. For Santayana, philosophers should attend to their own meditations. Only so will those meditations bear fruit that might be beneficent for others. For the other American classical philosophers, each member of the community, including the philosopher, is saved by saving the others.

Santayana's thought is a critical contrast to the mainstream of American classical philosophy. The terms of discourse are the same, but the results are entirely different. Rather than deliverance and dedication to the community there is benevolent neutrality toward it. Instead of the need to join with others and to be one of them, there is the disposition to keep a distance from others and to be different. Perhaps Santayana's thought was conditioned by his marginality to the New England society where he spent his youth and early adulthood. Perhaps the condition of not fitting into the community life around him was sublimated into the affirmation of his separateness by a process of Nietzschean *ressentiment*. Santayana, who was a skilled literary psychologist and a strict naturalist, would not have despised such reflections, but surely would have added that the American puritan philosophers were just as bound to their circumstances as he was. Perhaps he had gotten off easy and the necessity of leading his "inner life" alone was a blessing and not a curse. The other American classical philosophers were unable even to acknowledge that they were not entirely parts of the "irresistible crowd." Royce was perplexed by the wilderness of reflection, Peirce put his shoulder to the wheel perfecting a logical tool, James willed himself desperately into the community, and Dewey apprised us of the fact that we are all in the same boat. Each one had to make good his speculative independence by showing that it would benefit everyone else. For Santayana, such a demand was simply impossible to fulfill and, therefore, involved those who responded to it in vital self-contradiction.

Despite his differences from the other American classical philosophers, Santayana was united with them in the critique of the war-spirit, which he called "militancy" and "fanaticism." He traced the war-spirit, just as Royce had done, to the primal affirmation of the vital will, and found the root of immorality to be egotism. Both the life of reason, the harmonization of diverse goods in a single frame of life, and spiritual freedom, the dispassionate contemplation of the data presented in intuition, are destroyed by the militant effort to make a single good or a narrow set of goods supreme over all others. In the sphere of thought, fanaticism is epitomized by the pathetic fallacy through which the special wishes and interests of a thinker are projected onto reality, while in the sphere of action, militancy is most extreme when one group attempts to impose its way of living upon others or to annihilate the others because they are different. In his late work, particularly in *Dominations and Powers,* published in 1951, Santayana described the utopia of a "rational government," the aim of which would be "to prevent conflicting desires from becoming material conflicts, fatal to both sides."[19] Such a government would be run by technocrats and its authority would be "autocratic but not totalitarian; for it would speak for the material conditions imposed by nature on the realization of any ideal without dictating to any person or society what its ideal should be." The police in the service of a rational government would see to it that "the hot bloods and the ambitious talents" confined themselves to preaching and working for reforms in "the separate irrational rival forms of culture," and did not hurt anyone.

Rational government was, for Santayana, not a program, but a critical idea against which to measure how "reasonably actual governments behaved." Santayana's more fundamental position with regard to moral community is tragic. In *Character and Opinion in the United States* he contrasts English liberty, which he believes characterizes American life, with absolute liberty. The principle of English liberty is the maintenance of each individual's freedom through the compromise and cooperation of all. According to Santayana, its practice presupposes that "all concerned are fundamentally unanimous, and that each has a plastic nature, which he is willing to modify." These presuppositions are unfounded when individuals or groups claim the absolute liberty to express their particular potentials unhindered by any limitations. Santayana notes that a "free government" demands a society in which no interest is "carried so far as to lose sight of the rest: . . . The variety and distinction allowed must be only variety and distinction of service. If they ever become a real distinction and variety of life, if they arrogated to themselves an absolute liberty they would shatter the unity of the democratic spirit and destroy its moral authority." Yet Santayana cannot give his full assent to English liberty, because "co-operative life is reasonable and long-winded; but it always remains imperfect itself, while it somewhat smothers the impulses that enter into it." The suppression and collapse of absolute liberty is, in fact, a "deep tragedy," because "the narrower passions and swifter harmonies are more beautiful and perfect than the chaos and dull broad equilibrium that may take their place." Absolute liberty is the creator of the elements organized by English liberty, and "nothing good could arise for cooperation to diffuse or to qualify unless first there had been complete liberty for the artist and an uncontaminated perfection in his work." Santayana's idea of rational government resolves the tension between self-expression and cooperation because it represents things, not people. The contemporary mass democracy is a system for representing groups and individuals, and it is endangered both by the tyranny of homogenization and by factionalization into militant parts. The greatest threat to a democratic system is that factionalization will lead to the victory of one of the militant groups, which will rule not by the authority of things, but by the enchantment of a fantasy. Santayana did not give concrete direction for mastering the tension of modern social life, but merely noted that "absolute liberty and English liberty are incompatible, and mankind must make a painful and a brave choice between them." He concluded *Character and Opinion in the United States* with the observation that "the necessity of rejecting and destroying some things that are beautiful is the deepest curse of existence."[20]

Santayana's tragic vision is informed by his materialist conception of the frame of things, which prohibits him from the emphasis on will that is involved in William James's concept of inward tolerance. It is, in fact, contradictory for Santayana to speak of "mankind" making a "painful and brave choice" between English liberty and absolute liberty, because, for his naturalism, both "choice" and "mankind" are figments of literary psychology. Santayana's tragic view does, however, reveal that what sustained the political thought of Royce, Peirce, and Dewey was "Anglo-Saxon piety," a "mystical conviction" that "our labours, even when they end in failure, contribute to some ulterior achievement in which it is well they should be submerged."[21] For this piety Santayana thought to substitute another rooted in "a certain shrewd orthodoxy which the sentiment and practice of laymen maintain everywhere." But this "orthodoxy," which Santayana defined for himself, was no more than another over-belief, which he could know in advance would not be adopted by "the hot bloods and the ambitious talents." And he was often ready to concede that they should not adopt it, because it was not their nature to do so. Thus, Santayana himself lived within the tension between vital liberty and spiritual freedom. As a particular life he urged what he thought to be beneficial. As a free spirit he noted the virtues of each expression of nature. But the spirit's view, the tragic view, was closest to his heart. He shared the universe of discourse of the other American classical philosophers, but not their "Anglo-Saxon piety," and, therefore, he was able to make that piety stand out by creating a system of thought in which it was absent. But Santayana developed the full implications of his truncated system only after he left the United States and was able to interpret its life and thought from a vantage point in Europe. His gaze from afar picked out the problem that American society and philosophy would confront when Anglo-Saxon piety was discredited, but he gave that problem a tragic interpretation and, therefore, no resolution. By his own testimony he might not have been able to be so detached and dispassionate had he spent all his life as a thinker philosophizing in America.

7

American Philosophy and Modern Individualism

The development of American classical philosophy is the history of the encounter of a group of thinkers with the "death of God" in the West. In the late nineteenth century, throughout the Western world, a second wave of romanticism swept over the established civilization, washing away much of the remaining confidence in traditional life-commitments. The line of modern individualism, which was initiated by Martin Luther and René Descartes, and which was infused with romanticism by Jean-Jacques Rousseau, culminated in Friedrich Nietzsche's tragic vitalism. Nietzsche's "transvaluation of values," which Josiah Royce believed was the greatest cultural threat to civilization, placed in doubt all commitment to ideals transcending the individual life. Nietzsche's challenge to the educated groups in the West was to affirm life in its completeness, not merely in some of its happier phases. According to Nietzsche, the Western intellectual desired to maintain a scientific world picture, which included the Darwinian version of evolution, but not to accept concretely the moral consequences of that vision. Thus, for Nietzsche, the ruling and middle classes of the West were in bad faith, persuading themselves that they could have their positivism and also their salvation. Nietzsche's announcement that God was dead was aimed at the "half-and-half-ers," who believed that despite their destruction of the idols that had protected the city they could still be assured of the protection that belief in those idols had brought.

Nietzsche had gone into the wilderness and found that God had departed, leaving only the abyss. He drew the conclusion that if there is no God of the wilderness there is also no God of the city. The God of the city is, for Nietzsche, a creation of the vast number of weaker human beings who wish to hide from themselves the knowledge that they are finite and failed life. In *The Anti-Christ* Nietzsche notes that "Descartes was the first who, with a boldness worthy of reverence, ventured to think of the animal as a *machine:* our whole science of physiology is devoted to proving this proposition." Descartes, however, excluded human beings from the rule of mechanism. Nietzsche's task is to show that the unfolding of modern thought makes such a special status for human phenomena impossible to uphold in good faith: "Nor, logically, do we exclude man, as even Descartes did: our knowledge of man today is real knowledge precisely to the extent that it is knowledge of him as a machine."[1] According to Nietzsche, the mechanistic interpretation of nature reinterprets will as "a resultant, a kind of individual reaction which necessarily follows a host of partly contradictory, partly congruous stimuli—the will no longer 'effects' anything, no longer 'moves anything.' " In the absence of any belief in "free will" and "spirit" Nietzsche takes the viewpoint of a naturalist and evaluates human life according to its vitality. He observes that human beings are "absolutely not the crown of creation" and that, "relatively speaking," they are the most unsuccessful animals, the sickliest, and the ones "most dangerously strayed" from their instincts, although they are assuredly "the most *interesting.*" For Nietzsche, one of the aspects of world-sickness is self-loathing and self-hatred over the infirmities of the species which are revealed to human beings by their own science. The hatred of existence that may arise from the vision of an empty wilderness, a desert of the soul, breeds the tendency toward nihilism. Such nihilism may take the forms of severe *acedia,* leading to suicide, or to the war-spirit, which is revealed in its essence as the passion of the weak to trample the weak. Suicide and murder grow out of the same root of the denial of life. The first one is a rebellion against life by withdrawal from it and the second is a rebellion by an attempted imperialism over it.

Nietzsche did not reach his insight into the depth of the modern spiritual crisis created by individualism easily. In his early work, *The Birth of Tragedy,* he conducts "the sympathetic reader to a mountain peak of lonely contemplation" where he discourses on the essentiality of myth to the life of a people. Before the ancient Greeks began to view themselves "historically" and "to demolish the mythical bulwarks" that surrounded them, they had "felt an instinctive need to relate their experience at once to their myth, indeed to understand it only through that connection." Through their spontaneous bond with a timeless myth "even the immediate present appeared to them *sub specie aeternitatis.*" Their polis and their art were submerged in a "timeless stream" and they found "respite from the burden and the avidity of the immediate moment." Nietzsche concludes from his interpretation of Greek life that "a nation, like an individual, is valuable only insofar as it is able to give to quotidian experience the stamp of the eternal: . . . Only by so doing can it express its profound, if unconscious, conviction of the relativity of time and the metaphysical meaning of life." When a nation loses its myth it becomes enslaved to the rush of time and breaks its unity with the cosmos. The myth is the concrete link of the people to reality, the expression of their own relation to being, their native piety. A sense of history brings with it the relativity of perspectives, the uncertainty about which commitments should be made, and "the greedy rush to alien tables, the frivolous apotheosis of the present or the stupefied negation of it." Remarking that the entire modern period is similar to the era of Greek decadence, Nietzsche appeals to the German to recover mythic roots and "to listen to the call of the Dionysiac bird, which hovers above his head and will show him the way."[2]

The early Nietzsche retained many of the features of idealistic life-philosophy in his thought. Although he renounced the absolute mind in favor of the Dionysiac spirit "which playfully shatters and rebuilds the teeming world of individuals," at a deeper level of belief he affirmed the mystical vision of the consecration of the present moment and the idea of community as the end of individuated life. His program was one of cultural revival, "a true 'recovery' of all things German" and the challenge of becoming worthy of such "great predecessors" as Luther and "our best artists and poets." The later Nietzsche, in contrast, understood that the nihilistic disease had become far too acute in the West to be cured by a return to roots. He made a bold attempt in *Thus Spake Zarathustra* to provide a mythology consistent with Darwinism in order to stimulate a renewal of vitality in a declining culture dominated by positivistic assumptions. Rather than looking backward to a recovery of ancestral myth, Zarathustra looked forward to the creation of the over-man who would affirm finite existence with dignity and grace. For the later Nietzsche the city itself had been destroyed and had been claimed by the herd. There was no space for Zarathustra. The mountain peak was lonely and barren, but the plains were overrun by the herd, whose life was devoted to the mutual reassurance of and by its members that weakness was strength and that evil was good. In Nietzsche's thought the germ of hatred for existence, loathing of the other, and self-disgust, which was present in William James's vision of the epileptic during his episode of panic fear, blossomed into a rank weed. The heroic struggle of Nietzsche's life was to tolerate sheer species being, which had been glorified by the idealistic worship of culture and the positivistic worship of society. Having stripped away nineteenth-century progressive piety, Nietzsche was left with actual, individuated, and radically imperfect human life. He found it difficult, if not impossible, to stomach an unveiled humanity, from which he could not separate himself.

In Nietzsche's thought the death of God and the discovery of the abyss should not be separated from the confrontation with the positivity of finite, incarnated, and thoroughly vulnerable and diseased humanity. Nietzsche did not leave succeeding European thinkers merely with a void or a vacancy, which they might try to throw a rope over, but with a vision of human beings as constitutively diseased and mendacious animals; diseased by their own standards of health and mendacious by their own standards of truth. Nietzsche was far more a critic than a creator. He revealed the image of humanity implicit in nineteenth-century progressivism and historicism, and then devised measures to keep up vitality in spite of the compulsion of that image over the mind. The vision, implicit in Nietzsche's thought, of society as an immense sickroom without doctors—in which the diseased beg one another for cures but are only further infected—haunted later European thought. The possibility that hatred for existence might run even deeper than *acedia* was exploited by Jean-Paul Sartre in *Nausea*. In his famous vision of the roots of the chestnut tree, Sartre's protagonist, Antoine Roquentin, recounts that existence was revealed to him as "soft, monstrous masses, all in disorder—naked, in a frightful, obscene nakedness." Roquentin realized then "that there was no half-way house between non-existence and this flaunting abundance:... If you existed, you had to *exist all the way*, as far as mouldiness, bloatedness, obscenity were concerned." Roquentin's realization means, for him, that the "nausea" which he has felt for months is not "an illness or a passing fit: it is I."[3] Roquentin, no more than Nietzsche, is able or willing to exercise a "will to believe," to leap over the abyss, leaving the "sick soul" behind in the domain of "theory" and constituting a new self in the realm of "practical reasoning." European thinkers in the first half of the twentieth century won their positions either by passing through the trial that Nietzsche had instituted or by avoiding it conspicuously. American philosophers got off more easily. Their greatest spirit, William James, closed his eyes and leaped over the abyss, landing, as far as anyone could see, safely on the other side.

The judgment of European existentialists on American classical philosophy is summed up in Karl Jasper's statement in *Man in the Modern Age* that "pragmatism seemed to be laying new foundations; but what it built thereon was nothing more than an aggregate of crude analysis of life and cheap optimism, was a mere expression of blind confidence in the extant confusion."[4] The preceding chapters have shown that Jaspers's severe judgment is unfounded. The idealistic representatives of American classical philosophy, Royce and Peirce, did not present crude analyses of life or purvey cheap optimism, but were devout and questioning thinkers who, though they did not reconcile faith and reason successfully, made contact with and expressed eloquently the sources of positive mysticism. Similarly, the American naturalists, Dewey and Santayana, were acutely aware of the limitations of human existence, though they tried to provide consolation for them. And James, who stands at the midpoint between idealism and naturalism, provided as profound an insight into human existence as any European thinker. The analysis of life that he undertook in "The Sentiment of Rationality" was as complex and deep in its disclosure of an ontological dimension to speculative thought as that of European existentialism, and the optimism that he promoted was won desperately from the jaws of panic fear.

Yet the American classical philosophers fell short of their European counterparts in two respects: they did not acknowledge the radical separation of the philosopher from others and from the flux of life itself, and they did not think through to its conclusion, as Nietzsche did, the moral consequences of the death of God. Neither Royce nor Peirce, who were nineteenth-century visionaries, can be judged severely for failing to take account of radical separation or for failing to glimpse humanity as Nietzsche did. The severe judgment, paradoxically, falls heaviest on the greatest and most profound of the American life-philosophers, William James, because he was not a mystic and because he did glimpse all that Nietzsche tried to hold steady in his sight. Dewey and Santayana, though they evince what Royce called "vicious naïveté," are most appropriately interpreted as consequences of James's failure to peer into the abyss long enough. James's resort to the "will to believe" allowed the issue of life-philosophy in America to be diverted from the death-of-God problematic to the question of how best to live in the truth. Dewey and Santayana could in good conscience critique James for substituting success for truth. They could concentrate their attention on countering the irrationalism of the "will to believe" and sidestep encountering the nothingness of "ontological wonder-sickness." James's resort to a special realm of "practical reasoning" was, indeed, the best diversionary tactic he could have invented for blinding other American philosophers to the existentialist insights, concepts, and arguments that abound in his works.

The outstanding characteristic of American life-philosophy, which stamps even Santayana's thought, is its moral bias. Santayana noted in *Character and Opinion in the United States* that the deepest thing in Royce's personality was "conscience, firm recognition of duty, and the democratic and American spirit of service." Hegel or Nietzsche, Santayana observed, could adopt a moral bias "histrionically," but "the good Royce was like a sensitive amateur, refusing the role of villain, however brilliant and necessary to the play." Santayana, too, refused to play the role of villain and, at his best, moralized like a professional, cultivating a sense of sacrifice and a respect for "the authority of things." Santayana traced the moral bias of American classical philosophy to the fact that its institutional seedbed, Harvard University, had been "founded to rear puritan divines, and as Calvinism gradually dissolved, it left a void there and as it were a mould, which a philosophy expressing the same instincts in a world intellectually transformed could flow into and fill almost without knowing it."[5] The dissolution of

Calvinism occurred at the same time that Harvard, "a local puritan college," was "opening its windows to the scientific world." Thus, according to Santayana, its two "most gifted philosophers," Royce and James, combined attention to "the facts of nature and the currents of worldly opinion" with "religious and romantic feelings." In Santayana's view, Royce and James felt bound by the dual task of describing things as they were and of "finding them propitious to certain preconceived human desires."

Santayana's analysis surely accounts for Royce's overt project, which was to show the compatibility between "theoretic philosophy" (the effort to find out about the "real world") and "religious philosophy" (the search for an inspiring truth). It also helps in understanding Peirce's program, which included the affirmation of the reality of, though not the existence of, the absolute. But Santayana's analysis fails to comprehend James's thought, which did not find things "propitious to certain preconceived human desires" and which acknowledged the contingency of human experience. Further, Santayana's interpretation is relevant to the preoccupation of American philosophers with over-beliefs about the cosmos, but not to the moral bias of these over-beliefs, including his own defense of "a certain shrewd orthodoxy which the sentiment and practice of laymen maintain everywhere." Santayana's judgment that what was deepest in Royce was his conscience, recognition of duty, and spirit of service explains the limitations of Santayana's conclusion that American classical philosophy was based on the self-contradictory project of reconciling science and religion. Deeper than the superficial struggle between science and religion, which, as Nietzsche noted, had been won by science at the inception of the modern era, was the effort of American philosophers to center life-philosophy in moral commitment, an effort that may, indeed, have been a continuation of the puritan spirit. The moral theme in American classical philosophy appears nowhere as clearly as in James's claim at the conclusion of "The Will to Believe" that deliberate and profound respect for the mental freedom of others is supreme over the demands of any "conception of the frame of things."

The severest criticism that can be leveled against American classical philosophy is not that it was based on the pathetic fallacy, but that it did not think through morality seriously enough. When the consequences of the death of God are squarely faced and absorbed into life, no substitutes for God, whether cultural, social, or psychological are acceptable. There can no longer be, as Nietzsche understood, any taken-for-granted mediations between one human being and another. Each one faces the other starkly as a finite life in the process of corruption and as a center of an absolute demand against being that cannot be met. On the other side of the abyss there is, indeed, as James understood, the moral will, but that will can only be exerted purely if it is grounded in tolerance of the other not as a "rational being" or as an "imperfect logical being" or as a fragment of humanity, but as a finite and individuated life who is here and now an absolute center of expression and demand. It is an approximation of this image of the individual that is the context of Jean-Paul Sartre's apothegm that "hell is the other person." Those who have held in their gaze Nietzsche's vision of a sick humanity, who have been attentive to the real persons around them, may sigh with relief when they encounter someone who is devoted to a benign cause, but they cannot dedicate themselves to fostering the "will to believe." There are far too many malign causes for that and there is far too little inner tolerance. The gazer at humanity must work as hard at keeping up inner tolerance as the gazer at the abyss must work to hold fast to the flimsy veil of lived experience as though it were as durable and fecund as Santayana's substance. James, who is the heart and soul of American classical philosophy, was correct that the acknowledgment of nothingness is the gateway to empiricism and that inner tolerance is empiricism's glory. He defined in those observations the ground principles toward which Royce and Peirce blindly struggled and from which Dewey and Santayana fled. There is a sense in which the naturalists were more bound than the other American classical philosophers by the dual project of describing things as they were and of "finding them propitious to certain preconceived human desires." Their defenses of natural piety were primarily a way of making finitude palatable by the old measure of accentuating the positive and eliminating the negative.

The moral theme in American classical philosophy is expressed in the successive appeals for deliverance to the community and in the parallel critiques of the war-spirit. The idea of community performed the same function in American philosophy as the appeal to particularistic mythology performed in Nietzsche's early thought. In both cases a transpersonal and collective idea was devised to mediate between concrete human beings and to unite them in a common task. As Nietzsche's work matured and his terrifying insight grew clearer he became ever more impatient with symbolic unifications of human life. The American classical philosophers did not evince such impatience, but persisted in committing themselves to constructing beliefs about the nature of things that would stimulate moral conduct. From a Nietzschean viewpoint the function of an idea of social organization that mediates between human beings is to disguise the actuality and the concrete particularity of the others so that we do not have to encounter them as they are and ourselves as we are. Deliverance to the community, the central life-commitment of American classical philosophy, prescribes the devotion of the self to a task or a project through which others are served and not to the care of any particular others. The philosopher, for example, has the task of providing the community with beliefs about the cosmos that will encourage moral conduct. Self, then, is not relevant to concrete others but to a social whole, the maintenance and improvement of which depends upon the performance of certain roles. The American classical philosophers wisely left the precise definitions of the specific roles required to the social sciences and confined themselves to bolstering loyalty. The community was an abstract totality of voluntary servants who were bound to the social whole, not to the divinity. Here is the design of American classical philosophy, excluding Santayana's thought: the Christian idea of discipleship to the Lord is transferred to service to society.

The solution of American classical philosophy to the spiritual problems created by the death of God in the West was the substitution of society for God as the object of life-commitment, deliverance, discipleship, and service. The idealistic representatives of the American tradition still gave a divine sanction to the community, arguing, as Royce did, that the social whole is constitutive of the cosmos, or, as Peirce did, that the social whole is an idea that imposes itself on the mind as an object to be realized by the will. In the cases of both Royce and Peirce, the community is an aspect of divinity and permits mystical contact with the cosmos. For Royce, being, if properly interpreted, is a universal church, and, for Peirce, existence is the field for the creation of a universal church. James gave a new turn to the theme of deliverance to society by making it a moral commitment to serve an absolute demander

and not a devotion to an actual or probable eternal life. The idealists did not have to face the issue of loathing for the other person,
because they viewed each individual as a fragment of the divine.
James, in contrast, was aware of human attitudes under the
shadow of God's death: "Our attitude towards concrete evils is entirely different in a world where we believe there are none but finite demanders, from what it is in one where we joyously face
tragedy for an infinite demander's sake."[6] Dewey's naturalism did
not reach the depth of James's voluntaristic interpretation of commitment, but replaced the mystical visions of Royce and Peirce
with the insight that we are all in the same boat. According to
Dewey we should strive to make the boat as seaworthy as possible
and to direct it toward the most bounteous islands. In his thought,
society, interpreted as the totality of humanity, is divested of any
transcendent sanctification and made a secular alternative to
divinity.

The hallmark of American life-philosophy is a moral and a social
solution to a religious and a spiritual crisis. The great denial of
American classical philosophy is the denial of the separate self
who withdraws from participation in the common life. The self is
only realized, according to the American tradition, in discipleship
to the community. Separation of the self from the community is
self-contradictory and, in a certain sense, impossible, because, at
least for Royce, Peirce, and Dewey, and often even for James, the
separate self is an illusion. Royce's dictum that "my life means
nothing, either theoretically or practically unless I am a member
of a community" is the ground principle of the puritan strand of
American life-philosophy. James, in his flight from panic fear and
in his effort to reduce ontological wonder-sickness, which individ-
ualizes the human being radically, to a theoretical perplexity, embraces Royce's spirit and sometimes his letter. Peirce, of course, is
as severe a critic of the separate self as Royce, claiming that a human being is "essentially a possible member of society," and that
"it is not 'my' experience, but 'our' experience that has to be
thought of." Dewey, whose thought is the culmination of the puritan line, interprets the individual as a link in "the continuous human community." The devotion of American classical philosophers to the community is of religious significance. Human beings
are not merely wrong to separate themselves from the social
whole, but they violate their very being. Royce, Peirce, and Dewey

do not offer descriptions of the sick souls who rebel against their social origin and destiny, but instead confine themselves to urging loyalty when their ontologies imply that there should be no need to do so. The separate self is an embarrassment to their social faith, because they do not have an interpretation of sin. The consequence of a secular religion that lacks the idea of sin is Peirce's conclusion that "he who would not sacrifice his own soul to save the whole world is . . . illogical."

The theme of deliverance to the community is counterbalanced in American classical philosophy by the critique of the war-spirit, which was undertaken by all the great American thinkers, including Santayana. The steady and principled opposition of American philosophers to fanaticism is their lasting and important contribution to life-philosophy, and is the key to what is vital and what may be carried forward in the American tradition. The critique of the war-spirit appears in American classical philosophy as a means of defending the integrity of a universal community, but the critique implies a virtue that is not present in the mere ideas of deliverance, discipleship, and service. That virtue, of course, is James's inner tolerance of difference, which depends upon forebearance or what Heidegger called "letting-be." The "delicate and profound" respect for the mental freedom of others that James advocated at the conclusion of "The Will to Believe" is the basis of a social order in which self-control substitutes for social control and in which the abstractly universal community becomes a free community of actual persons. Self-control, however, depends upon reserve and not upon enthusiasm. It requires an inner discipline of self-limitation rather than a deliverance of oneself to a greater life. The American classical philosophers did not think through their critiques of the war-spirit and develop an adequate analysis of self-control because they put so much stock in the power of over-beliefs and in the spirit of service. The symbolic mediations that they constructed between human beings disguised the corrosive intolerance at the heart of the late modern era.

Irving Babbitt, an American thinker of the same generation as Dewey and Santayana, who was educated at and taught at Harvard, devoted his thought to the possibilities for self-control in contemporary societies. Babbitt, the founder of neo-humanism and a critic of mass democracy, was not a professional philosopher, but was a literary critic who enlarged the discipline of criticism to include the most comprehensive speculative concerns. His thought deserves consideration in an analysis of American classical philosophy, not only because his terms of discourse are the same as those of Royce, Peirce, James, Dewey, and Santayana, but because his position on life-commitment is in such contrast to theirs, and shows the limitations of mainstream puritanism. Babbitt's conception of criticism is decidedly philosophical and is derived from Matthew Arnold's idea of "a criticism of life." Walter Jackson Bate notes that Babbitt "revolutionized the approach to the history of literary criticism: . . . It was no longer viewed as a series of opinions or expressions of taste but as an articulation of more central attitudes."[7] Harry Levin, who calls Babbitt "the voice of reason that cried out so passionately in a wilderness of distractions," observes that he "was fundamentally a moralist, like the Existentialists of today; like them he sought a metaphysical groundwork for his ethics."[8] J. David Hoeveler, Jr., who considers Babbitt to be "the dominant mind in the Humanist movement," argues that "placing the intellectual outline of the New Humanists within the context of contemporary philosophical currents makes it possible to show to what extent the Humanists moved against the prevailing currents of thought and to suggest also how their own campaign was a response to these." As Hoeveler shows, just when Dewey was attacking philosophical dualism, Babbitt was upholding a dualistic perspective in self-conscious opposition to the pragmatists.[9] Babbitt, then, stressed an approach to life-philosophy that emphasized modes of possibility different from those that the other American classical philosophers did; his was a commitment to restraint, not to deliverance.

Babbitt's thought is brought forward here, at the conclusion of the present study of American classical philosophy, not as an alternative to the mainstream ideas but as a supplement to them. His emphasis on the uniquely interior and irreducible act of self-control as the basis of moral life provides a firmer ground (one based in direct personal experience) for avoiding the slide into *acedia* or into the war-spirit than the effort to create a benign object for collective enthusiasm does. The neo-humanist idea that the focus of individual existence should be the war in Plato's cave, the struggle between desire and restraining will, is an important corrective to preoccupation with Dewey's arts of external control.

Recent commentary, such as Levin's and Hoeveler's, has moved beyond the "battle of the books" which took place between neo-humanist and progressive critics during the interwar period and which, often through Babbitt's own rhetorical excesses, sharpened and rigidified the choices between self-control and control over external nature, and between attachment to permanent features of existence and attention to mutable aspects of reality. Hoeveler, indeed, argues that Dewey's interpretation of the permanent and the fixed as "merely ratios of change in an unstable flux of experience" converges with neo-humanist thought.[10] With regard to life-philosophy, the act of self-restraint is not opposed to the virtues urged by the mainstream thinkers but is instead the fundamental guarantor of James's inner tolerance: it is the drawing back from immediate discharge of an impulse which creates the time for tolerance to deepen. The bitter struggles that occurred after World War I between the partisans of Babbitt's Burkean conservatism and the advocates of Dewey's liberalism should not hinder acknowledgment and appropriation of Babbitt's uniquely important contribution to the classical discourse of American life-philosophy.

Babbitt's chief work in life-philosophy is *Rousseau and Romanticism*, which Hoeveler calls "the most important work of the New Humanism."[11] Published in 1919, it is a critique of the "Rousseauistic philosophy of life" and a defense of the thesis that "the total tendency of the Occident at present is away from rather than towards civilization."[12] Babbitt's project in *Rousseau and Romanticism*, most generally, was to counterpose what he called the *frein vital*, or "inner check," against the *élan vital* or "expansive emotion." He believed that the thought and the sensibility of the contemporary era were ruled by "romanticism," by which he meant the doctrine commending the spontaneous and unchecked expression of feeling. In opposition to romanticism he defended a new classicism, which was based on a reworking of the ideas of "decorum," "probability," and "imitation," which dominated eighteenth-century classicism, and an application of these ideas to concrete life.

Babbitt's contribution to the discourse on life-commitment of American classical philosophy was a dualistic life-philosophy, defended in opposition to both the monistic visions of the idealists and the naturalists, and the pluralistic conception of James's empiricism. Babbitt grounded his dualism on an attempt to think through a "complete positivism" and to adopt what he called the "modern spirit" without reservation. The "negative side" of Babbitt's argument was directed "against the attempt to erect on naturalistic foundations a complete philosophy of life," while "on the positive side" he aimed "to reassert the 'law for man,' and its special discipline against the various forms of naturalistic excess." Babbitt defined the modern spirit as "the positive and critical spirit, the spirit that refuses to take things on authority," and held that a "complete positivist" would affirm, on the basis of a thorough examination of experience, "the duality of human nature" and the existence of a distinctively "human law" separate from the natural laws discovered by the experimental sciences. According to Babbitt, the intellectual error of the modern age was "incomplete positivism." He maintained that when traditional authorities were discredited in the early modern era European intellectuals did not meet the challenge of creating a critical authority to take their place, but, instead, let moral thought drift into an apotheosis of sentiment. Babbitt declared himself to be an individualist, defining the core of individualism to be planting oneself "not on outer authority but on experience." He defined "the specifically modern problem" as "the establishment of a sound type of individualism."[13]

Babbitt states that in order to be a "sound individualist" in an age "that has cut loose from its traditional moorings," one "must grapple with what Plato terms the problem of the One and the Many." He follows Plato in affirming an immediate perception of "an element of unity in things," but breaks with Platonic thought by refusing to establish "a world of essences or 'ideas' above the flux." Babbitt's general solution to the "problem of the One and the Many," then, is to uphold the Platonic intuition of the idea of the good, but to dispense with the realm of forms which, for Plato, mediated between the intuition of unity and the sensory flux. Thus, Babbitt does not base his neo-classicism on the intellectual intuition of essences, which he asserts is a doctrine contrary to the "positive and critical attitude," and one more consistent with a "speculative attitude." He seeks his ground, instead, in the direct experience of life which reveals *"a oneness that is always changing."* It is Babbitt's certitude about a unity in the flux that backs up his critique of "thinkers like James and Bergson and Dewey and

Croce," whom he accuses of building up "their own intoxication
with the element of change into a complete view of life, and so are
turning their backs on one whole side of experience in a way that
often reminds one of the ancient Greek sophists."[14]

Babbitt's spirit is actually far more mystical, in the sense of the
ascetic mysticism of the Orient, than it is rationalistic. He is suspicious of all fixed ideas and seeks a mediation between the One and
the Many in the imagination and not in logical reason. Drawing
upon the ancient Indian idea of the veil of appearance, Babbitt
claims that "life is at best a series of illusions" and that, therefore,
"the whole office of philosophy is to keep it from degenerating into
a series of delusions." From a strictly logical viewpoint, it does not
appear possible for Babbitt to distinguish between illusion and
delusion, because both terms refer to erroneous judgments and
he provides no standard of truth. However, Babbitt attempts to
show that illusion can be distinguished from delusion by differen-
tiating the "concentric" and the "eccentric" imaginations. The
concentric imagination is directed to "the supreme and perfect
Centre that Dante glimpses at the end of the 'Divine Comedy,' "
while the eccentric imagination "owes allegiance to nothing above
itself" and runs "the risk of taking some cloud bank for terra
firma." But the appeal to a "supreme and perfect Centre," the
vision of which, Babbitt says, strikes Dante "dumb," does not provide a criterion for separating cloud banks from terra firma. In
order to be consistent with his chaste mysticism, Babbitt must resort to a pragmatic test for determining truth within the flux, and
so he does. Arguing that the "true positivist" is inclined to dismiss
"the mechanistic view of nature" as a "phantasmagoria of the intellect," Babbitt remarks that "we do not know and can never
know what nature is in herself," though "we can pick up a practical and piecemeal knowledge of nature not by dreaming but by
doing." Not only science, however, but also the special human dimension that transcends the flux, is submitted by Babbitt to the
pragmatic test. He observes that the "sense of the gap between
man and nature seems to be more fully justified by its fruits in life
and conduct, and this is after all the only test that counts in the
long run."[15]

Babbitt is enabled to avoid William James's "ontological wonder-sickness" only because he contrasts the "world of pure experience" to a positive idea of the One rather than to a critical idea of

nothingness. From a Jamesian viewpoint, Babbitt's philosophy simply lacks the profundity of questioning the entirety of the immediately given, including the oneness that runs through change, against the background of the void. The belief in a unity of being supporting the flux is a metaphysical commitment, an over-belief, which cannot be sustained by even the most profound experience of centeredness, because such an experience is always subject to comparison with other experiences, for example, that of panic fear, in a reflexive review. A radical empiricism, as James understood, asserts positivity only against the background of negativity, and against that background the sheer facticity and contingency of experience on the whole become conspicuous. However, although Babbitt's ontology lacks depth, his ascetic mysticism of restraint allowed him to grasp that the problem of life-philosophy in the modern era is "the establishment of a sound type of individualism." Babbitt was the only one among the American thinkers fully to grasp Nietzsche's image of a humanity out of control, a herd that was wandering without guidance and that was tending toward hatred of existence. Babbitt differed from Nietzsche only in his interpretation of a critical positivism. For Nietzsche a complete positivism meant drawing out the moral consequences of the mechanistic world picture, whereas for Babbitt it meant repudiating mechanism and interpreting science in terms of positive mysticism.

Babbitt believed that the greatest threat to individualism in the modern period was the confidence in expansive emotion. He understood that the primal process of the expression of judgments is normless and that if a person surrenders to it, any sort of will may appear and any sort of conduct may be enacted: "The man who makes self-expression and not self-control his primary endeavor becomes subject to every influence." Babbitt's response to the rising tide of expansive emotion was a twofold appeal to what he called the "inner check" and to classical standards such as imitation, decorum, and probability. The inner check or the "power of vital control" is linked by Babbitt to "the immediate perception of a something anterior to both thought and feeling, that is known practically as a power of control over both." The "superrational intuition" both reveals and puts into operation a power that reverses the direction of the *élan vital* toward untrammeled self-expression and, thus, limits the discharge of impulse. The *frein vital*, however, is merely formal and must be supplemented by a content. Here Babbitt joins the "inner or human infinite" that is grasped by superrational intuition and manifested in the inner check to what he calls "true decorum." According to Babbitt, "true decorum is only the pulling back and disciplining of impulse to the proportionateness that has been perceived with the aid of what one may term the ethical or generalizing imagination." What is here called the "ethical or generalizing imagination" is what Babbitt had earlier termed the "concentric imagination." It is imagination that "unites the probable with the wonderful" and that, therefore, creates suitable models of conduct for imitation. A classical period in a civilization sets up such models against which individuals can measure their emotions and judgments, and, thus, unites human beings in a community transcending bonds of feeling. According to Babbitt the root flaw in romanticism is abandonment of the doctrine of imitation, because when this doctrine is overthrown the "eccentric imagination" is given free play and human beings are subject to enacting any possibility that appears to them: "According to Voltaire genius is only judicious imitation. According to Rousseau the prime mark of genius is refusal to imitate."[16] The concentric imagination functions to fix an image of human nature or a group of related images that defines what is normal in a moral and not merely in a statistical sense. The eccentric imagination defines its own standards for itself and is ruled merely by the desire to express itself. There is, of course, no limit on what it may express.

Babbitt fails to achieve a logical or even a phenomenological link between the formation of terms that include superrational intuition, the human infinite, and the inner check, and the formation that includes human law, true decorum, and the concentric imagination. The first set of terms defines an ascetic mysticism for which all images are merely illusions, whereas the second set defines a doctrine of natural law which differs from that of Western tradition only by being rooted in the imagination rather than in reason. The deeper impulse in Babbitt is toward the mysticism, though his contribution to American criticism was as a classicist who upheld natural law. Babbitt's mysticism is most evident in his discussion of the irony of civilization near the conclusion of *Rousseau and Romanticism*. He remarks that "a civilization that rests on dogma and outer authority cannot afford to face the whole truth about imagination and its role." However, "a civilization in which dogma and outer authority have been undermined by the critical spirit, not only can but must do this very thing if it is to continue at all." The irony is that although civilization "must rest on the recognition of something abiding," the truth is that human beings are "cut off from immediate access to anything abiding and therefore worthy to be called real, and condemned to live in an element of fiction or illusion." Human beings do not consent, according to Babbitt, to submit their imaginations to "the necessary control" and will discipline themselves only when "the truths that are symbolically true" are presented as "literally true." Yet civilization fosters the critical spirit that ultimately undermines the "credulity" necessary to sustain it. Babbitt does not believe that the cycle that leads to civilization's self-destruction is easily broken and notes that "the emancipation from credulous belief leads to an anarchic individualism that tends to destroy civilization." The only hope that he holds out is for the appearance of someone like Buddha who combines a critical sense of the "evanescence of all things" and stern ethical standards: "A man may safely go into himself if what he finds there is not, like Rousseau, his own emotions, but like Buddha, the law of righteousness."[17] As his final judgment Babbitt surrenders his program of classical reform and affirms ascetic discipline grounded in mysticism. The "inner check," itself made the object of concentration and will, yields an inward law of righteousness that follows from renunciation of the Many in favor of the One. The generalizing and ethical imagination has dropped from view and Babbitt's thought has drawn near to that of James and Nietzsche, both of whom, like Babbitt, were acutely aware of the "vital lie," the religious mythology that had sustained Western civilization, but that had been supplanted by the scientific world picture.

Babbitt is the major American thinker to have introduced turn-of-the-century cultural pessimism into the United States. He is similar to Santayana in the sense that he substituted for progressive ideals of infinite and universal community a more particularized commitment rooted in culture. Santayana's defense of common sense and of the "shrewd orthodoxy which the sentiment and practice of laymen maintain everywhere" is paralleled by Babbitt's appeal to the classical standards of decorum, proportion, and probability, all of which refer to a moral perspective on what is normal for human beings. And, just as Santayana's defense of common sense was more superficial than his impulse to spiritual freedom, Babbitt's classicism floated atop his deeper mysticism. Babbitt appears to have had the courage to affirm life despite its insubstantiality, though his emphasis on self-control hints at difficulties he may have had in suppressing some of his emotions. However, he either would not or could not abandon the American philosopher's vocation of moral educator and attempted to make his link with the community through a call for its members to live up to high standards.

The deepest irony, if not the tragedy, of Babbitt's classicism is that he affirmed it in a culture that he criticized for having repudiated the very notion of imitation in favor of uniqueness and originality at whatever cost. According to Babbitt, true decorum had to be based on the imitation of models that were relevant to the particular life of an era. But a romantic era had no models and just as Nietzsche had to renounce his plea for the renovation of German mythology, Babbitt had to back away from his promotion of classicism and retreat to an austere mysticism that could only serve to sustain a tiny elite. Babbitt's appeal to the "concentric" or "generalizing and ethical" imagination was formal, because he could not point to any contemporary examples of its exercise. He could only announce the need for a classical revival; he could not create, promote, or join one. Babbitt's importance for American classical philosophy is not his classicism or his mysticism, but his defense of self-control, which does, indeed, appear within experience as a power of attention that holds back the flood of spontaneous expression, demand, and act. The *frein vital* may not indicate a unity of being, as Babbitt thought it did, but it does indicate that another synthesis of self-assertion and self-denial is possible than the deliverance to a cause, which was what the mainstream puritan thinkers embraced.

Babbitt's defense of self-control was not undertaken primarily to foster a reform in the arts, but to counteract what he judged to be a severe moral decline in Western civilization. According to Babbitt, nineteenth-century optimism was superficial and masked a profound disillusionment with life. Tracing the implications of his thesis that the modern spirit had stopped halfway between a revolt against traditional authority and a fully critical affirmation of life, Babbitt argued that the nineteenth-century ideologies of progress had caused the masses of "half-educated" individuals to hope for the "benefits of communion" without "the yoke of any serious discipline." Thus, in the terms of the Protestant theologian Dietrich Bonhoeffer, the life-philosophies of the romantic era promised "cheap grace," or, as Babbitt puts it, the attainment of "salvation without conversion." The promise of cheap grace is, for Babbitt, false and inevitably disappoints the expectations of those who believe in it. The result of disappointment and disillusionment is, according to Babbitt, "romantic melancholy," the symptoms of which are a "sense of loneliness," "forlornness," and "solitude." Those who suffer from romantic melancholy are "ready to blame everyone and everything" except themselves for their plight. The root of romantic melancholy, however, is the "abrupt disappearance of the older forms of communion" and "the failure of the new attempts at communion." Here Babbitt compares the new sickness of the soul to *acedia*. Medieval Christianity considered "sluggishness and slackness of spirit," and mere "drifting and abdication of the will" to be the "supreme danger" to the soul. Victims of *acedia* felt "cut off from God and so ceased to strive." However, those who suffered from *acedia* could not detach themselves from the community so "as to suffer that sense of loneliness which is the main symptom of romantic melancholy." The difference between the medieval and the modern types of spiritual privation is that the former occurred within the context of a community and the latter is associated with separation from and resentment against other people.

As was noted in the second chapter of the present work, Josiah Royce's "religious philosophy" can be interpreted as an effort to overcome *acedia* through deliverance to community. Similarly, William James's judgment that it is easier to make sacrifices for an absolute demander than for finite demanders indicates that he grasped the moral dangers of spiritual privation. C. S. Peirce and John Dewey did not discuss "soul sickness" at great length, but they did criticize idleness severely. Peirce's critique of feigned doubting and Dewey's strictures against the "quest for certainty" were both directed to fostering active participation in improving the common life. The puritan line of American classical philosophers responded to the melancholy that Babbitt discerned in the modern era by attempting to revive communion. In the terms of Babbitt's analysis they failed, because they did not prescribe any inward discipline for sustaining communal relations, but merely made appeals for whole-hearted cooperation. From another viewpoint, however, the mainstream American philosophers made an appropriate response to their circumstances. The medieval community, according to Babbitt's interpretation, had been held together by religious symbols, particularly by each individual's relation to the same God. Thus, medieval *acedia* occurred within a community of faith. The victim of spiritual privation suffered anguish, but still had the possibility of reunion with God and, therefore, with the community. It was possible for and, indeed, probably required of the individual to participate in the external rituals whether or not genuine faith was present.

Modern melancholy, in contrast, is not a spiritual event within a community of faith, but a constitutive condition of personal life in a society that lacks a unifying faith. Under the shadow of the death of God, the American puritan philosophers projected ideal communities to be realized by the commitment of those who would create them. The idea of willed community is, of course, clearest in William James's posit of a moral order as the object of practical reason, but it is also evident in Peirce's regulative idealism and in Dewey's humanism. Even Royce, who believed that the infinite community is completed eternally in the absolute life, prescribed a commitment to the creation of community in the temporal order. There is a sense in which the response of the mainstream puritans was more profound than that of Babbitt: a community had to be created before the possibility of a discipline to sustain it could be explored. Of course, new communal bonds depended upon self-control, which in turn depended upon such bonds. The mainstream puritans did not provide the means for engendering solidarity out of its absence and thereby for providing a containment barrier against romantic melancholy, but neither did Babbitt. Both Babbitt and those whom he criticized were one sided. But even their one-sidedness is intelligible because speculation about the reconciliation of individual and society had to start with one of the two poles and hold the other relative to the favored one.

In Babbitt's view, *acedia* was the consequence of disillusionment and contained not only boredom and abdication of the will, but also bitterness against the world and particularly against other persons. Melancholy was not a primordial state of the human spirit for Babbitt, but was rather a result of the failure of the spirit to fulfill itself. Here Babbitt's interpretation of the denial of will is consistent with Royce's analysis of resignation. For Royce, resignation or abnegation of the will to live arises when naive affirmation of that will breaks against natural limitations. According to Royce, "primal solipsism" is inevitably frustrated because it is opposed by other wills. Opposition of wills generates mutual hatred, which may be overcome by resignation or by loyalty. The addition that Babbitt makes to Royce's dialectic is the claim that denial of the will to live, when it results from disillusionment, produces a resentment against "everyone and everything." By introducing resentment into his account of romantic melancholy, Babbitt makes contact with Nietzsche's perspective on the modern spirit. If the implications of the tendency to blame everyone and everything for the frustrations of the assertive will are traced to their conclusion, the result is the hatred for existence that Nietzsche believed to be the poison of modern life. Of all the American classical philosophers, Babbitt came closest to identifying the phenomenon of *ressentiment*, the rebellion against finite existence, in which the self conceals from itself its own self-hatred by detracting from others and from the world in general. *Ressentiment* is built on a false separation of the self from its inextricable relations to the world. The separation is false because it is undertaken in reaction to a prior and naive unity that indicates that human being is being-in-the-world. The separation from one's own existence presupposed by *ressentiment* is not the same as the radical separation from practicality undertaken by the philosopher. The separation that is necessary to grasp experience against the background of nothingness does not judge experience morally, but reveals all moral judgments to be practical. The separation presupposed by *ressentiment*, in contrast, does pass moral judgment on the world, and the judgment it passes is unfavorable. The *ressentiment* self only separates itself from existence sufficiently to hate it. But it does not allow itself to become aware of its self-hatred. Thus, the *ressentiment* self projects its self-hatred outward and blames everyone and everything for its plight.

The primordial expression of *ressentiment* is the will of the weak to trample over the weak. Even suicide, if the Nietzschean perspective is taken to its conclusion, is a sublimation of revulsion against the flesh of others that conceals revulsion against our own flesh. Babbitt stood aside from the Nietzschean experience by creating a realm of decorum and, ultimately, by embracing an ascetic mysticism that drew him away from raw life. From a Nietzschean viewpoint, Babbitt's humanism is an elegant sublimation of loathing for the flesh, an elaborate and rarified substitution for encountering the other person directly. For Babbitt, human being is primarily representative being. Each one, at best, achieves an approximation to perfection by the imitation of apt models. In the mutual encounter of individuals each one judges the others in accordance with how well they meet the standards instituted by the concentric imagination. The Nietzschean vision, in contrast, demolishes the fantasy of representative being by making each individual a center of demand against itself and against life who simultaneously struggles to affirm life. The severe trial of the "inner check" or of the *frein vital* is not the struggle to dam expansive emotion, but the struggle to overcome hatred of existence. On the other side of James's "pit of insecurity" is not the love of life, but, as he intimated, the inner tolerance for it. Such inner tolerance is a moral attainment, in the sense that it is the existential ground for moral conduct. It is not limited, as James seemed to confine it, to tolerance of ideas and expressions, but must go as deep as tolerance of the other person's inalienable and corrupted life. Inner tolerance, when given a radically naturalistic interpretation, demands the exercise of an inner check. The ground of that inner check cannot be a vision of one's potential nobility, but is more appropriately a hearty disgust at oneself, tempered by a smile, which it was Nietzsche's tragedy never to form.

Contemporary *acedia*, Babbitt's "romantic melancholy," is overcome, though imperfectly, by experiencing its existential foundations. It is evaded by all of the numberless ways devised by the weak to trample over the weak. The root of the war-spirit, which so horrified the American classical philosophers and against which they fought by constructing ideals of universal community, is the hatred for existence. Babbitt's version of the critique of the war-spirit comes the closest of those in American classical philosophy to getting at the basis of fanaticism, though it does not penetrate to existential hatred. Babbitt discusses the war-spirit in his general treatment of "romantic melancholy." He notes that "scientific determinism was responsible for a great deal of spiritual depression and *acedia*" during the second half of the nineteenth century and proposes an explanation for why science "does not deserve to be given the supreme and central place in life." According to Babbitt, scientific practice incorporates a healthy discipline to an order that is independent of the individual's "fancies and emotions." However, the objectivity cultivated in the natural sciences only gives control over "natural forces" and "does not supply the purpose for which these forces are to be used." Thus, science "disciplines man and makes him efficient on the naturalistic level, but leaves him ethically undisciplined." Babbitt claims that in the absence of ethical discipline the strongest of the expansive emotions, the "lust for power," reigns unchecked. The most "terrible peril" that results from the civilization's halt halfway between tradition and critical affirmation is "that most sinister of all types, the efficient megalomaniac." Babbitt warns that "the man who does not rein in his will to power and is at the same time very active according to the natural law is in a fair way to become an efficient megalomaniac." Anticipating the rise of totalitarianism and total warfare, Babbitt observes that efficient megalomania eventually leads to war. The mutual hatred, which Royce believed was the result of a frustrated will to live, leads in a scientific age, according to Babbitt, to mutual annihilation. He concludes: "The efficient megalomaniacs will proceed to destroy one another along with the material wealth to which they have sacrificed everything else; and then the meek, if there are any meek left, will inherit the earth."[18]

The concept of efficient megalomania gives a material dimension to fanaticism that is lacking in Royce's critique of the warspirit, Peirce's denunciation of the party spirit, James's strictures against intolerance, Dewey's criticism of zealous faith, and Santayana's critique of militancy. Dewey and Santayana, of course, were aware of the special danger to the continuance of civilization posed by modern technologies. Dewey's program of applying experimental method to the reconstruction of social life was deliberately aimed at fostering intelligent control of science and its applications, while Santayana's ideal of a "rational government" was intended to show how ideological conflicts might be kept from becoming material conflicts. Both Dewey and Santayana, however, were partisans of the natural sciences. Dewey believed that experimental method was constituted by an intrinsic morality of cooperation that could be a paradigm for all social relations, while Santayana believed that the natural sciences yielded the only knowledge of things attainable by human beings. Neither of them thought to limit scientific investigation or even to warn against its dangers. Science was basically beneficent for Dewey and Santayana, as it was for their predecessors Royce, Peirce, and James. For any of them to cast doubt on the desirability of the advance of scientific inquiry would have been, in their judgment, to put themselves on the side of obscurantism and reaction. Babbitt was surely not antiscientific, but he was a critic and, therefore, was not as influenced as the others, who were professional philosophers, by the scientific bias of the modern philosophical tradition. His position on the margins of philosophy enabled him to give a more complete critique of fanaticism than the other American classical thinkers.

The major limitation of Babbitt's account of efficient megalomania is its failure to analyze the lust for power sufficiently. The basic dialectic of the will, which is brought forward by Royce in his critique of Schopenhauer and which informs American life-philosophy, is structured by the three moments of unselfconscious affirmation of life, self-conscious separation from life, and self-conscious unity with life. The dialectic is most sharply etched in Royce's discussion where submission to a cause is made the dialectical synthesis between self-assertion and self-abnegation. However, this dialectic is implicit in the thought of the other American classical philosophers, none of whom, except perhaps Santayana, were willing to choose resignation explicitly. The ground assumption of the dialectic of the will, as it is developed in American classical philosophy, is that human beings seek a reconciliation with existence that includes a reconciliation with themselves, with the cosmos, and with other people. The aim of the American classical philosophers, including Santayana and Babbitt, was to discover the character of an adequate reconciliation. Their task presupposed that there were inadequate reconciliations, specifically those that evinced the war-spirit. The war-spirit, then, is not the result of an untrammeled will to power, which as Royce noted is solipsistic and naive, but of a radically distorted or perverted synthesis of self-assertion and self-abnegation. The naive lust for power is merely an assertion of what Royce called "primal solipsism" and what Santayana called "primal will." The primary assertion of life does not engender efficient megalomania because it has no awareness of the sacrifices required in order to be efficient. Deliberate fanaticism emerges when the "primal will"

has been disciplined by the "authority of things" and seeks to re-
store its former naive condition. This is the meaning that a depth
psychology that follows Nietzsche's lead gives to Royce's idea of
"vicious naïveté." The viciously naive are those who have suffered
the frustrations of finitude, who have been injured severely, but
who attempt to disguise from themselves the wounds that cannot
heal. They have confused the ontological order, in which all are
justified because all have been injured, with the moral order, in
which there is no justification for adding to injury. By an existential hatred, they pervert the moral order by claiming the justification to injure others.

What Babbitt calls the "lust for power" is actually the hatred for
existence, which at its depth is hatred for oneself, because the self
is at the center of its own existence. The great project of modern
times is, as Babbitt claimed, "the establishment of a sound type of
individualism." Another way of defining this project is to say that
modern individualism means claiming oneself as one's own or becoming responsible for one's life. The challenge of the modern
spirit is to give content to oneself and to one's responsibility by
passing through the trials instituted by those who have sought
self-knowledge and, if one is capable of doing so, by adding to
those trials. The paradox and irony of modern life and thought is
that at each step in its history the knowledge of the self that is revealed becomes more dangerous and the temptation to conceal
that knowledge becomes more compelling. The challenge for the
modern spirit today is to pass through Nietzsche's trial of world-
sickness. American culture, which is the last outpost of Western
individualism, has evaded Nietzsche's insight into the hatred of
human beings for their own existence when the veils of piety have
been lifted from their awareness. Among the American classical
philosophers only William James came close to the Nietzschean
phenomenology of the spirit, but he drew back in horror from reflection on his panic fear and chose to stimulate in other people a
will to believe. James shows most clearly how life-philosophy has
been conceived in America. It has been a means for helping people
to live from one day to the next, a way of inspiring participation in
the common life, and, above all, a way of accentuating the positive.
Yet the dialectic that structures American life-philosophy is in-
herited from the pessimist, Arthur Schopenhauer. The American
search for a reconciliation of the self with existence was under-

taken against Schopenhauer's counsel of resignation and with the will to overcome *acedia* and to struggle against the war-spirit. This deep structure of American life-philosophy is sound and is the only base to which a new individualism can repair for guidance. However, there cannot be a mere repetition of the American classical tradition today. The efficient megalomania against which Babbitt warned has worked its way into the center of American culture and will not be easily plucked out. Contemporary fanaticism feeds on the hatred for existence, proliferating weapons and poisons and wastes. The intolerance of existence has issued in the systematic erosion of the basis for life.

The basis for a renewal of individualism in the present day is a deepening of inner tolerance to the point at which it becomes normal and not eccentric to live with world-sickness and still to be free for commitment to limited tasks within the public domain. Inner tolerance is the synthesis that a radical naturalism forges between the assertion and the denial of the will, between the militant and the passive modes of intolerance. The gravest of evils today is the massive aggregation of the weak into organized complexes that trample on the disorganized weak. The "age of narcissism," as the decade of the 1970s has been termed, is only superficially one of self-concern and isolation. There has been in American culture during this decade abundant "romantic melancholy" and *acedia*, but there has been far more *ressentiment* and war-spirit, as compact groups have coalesced to push aside those who, in Sartre's words, are "in the way." There is a nearly universal sense of injury in America today, a will on the part of many to "get even." The sense of a "declining life" has spurred, as Nietzsche's analysis predicts, a bitterness that is often overt but that even more frequently hides behind a brittle piety. If ever the time was ripe for a return to the sound elements of the American tradition of life-philosophy it is now, particularly the critique of the war-spirit and the defense of self-control. An unillusioned individualism can count only on an "inner tolerance" and an "inner check" to preserve civil society from the rule of a militant collectivism. There is, of course, little chance that the modern spirit will survive the twentieth century. When modernity was innocent, those who aspired to be modern could believe that the liberation of the self as an absolute center of judgment would lead spontaneously to an enlightened harmony. We know too much about ourselves today to be optimists about human nature. A genuine individualism is no cheaper than a genuine Christianity was for Bonhoeffer, and, one might add, it is just as rare. Modern individualism may perish, not primarily because of changes in the material conditions of life, but because the self-knowledge upon which it must be based to keep good faith is too demanding, even for those who have trained themselves to be adepts in its pursuit. For several decades the American tradition of life-philosophy has been moribund. A renewal of individualism in America requires that this tradition be deepened and revitalized. The odds are slim, but, as James might say, the option is alive.

Notes

1 AMERICAN PHILOSOPHY AS A FORM OF MODERN PHILOSOPHY

1. Andrew Reck, *Introduction to William James* (Bloomington: Indiana University Press, 1964), p. 3.
2. Benjamin K. Rand, *Modern Classical Philosophers* (Boston: Houghton Mifflin Co., 1908), p. iii.
3. Martin E. Marty, *Varieties of Unbelief* (Garden City: Doubleday and Co., 1966), p. 103.
4. William A. Clebsch, *American Religious Thought: A History* (Chicago: University of Chicago Press, 1973), pp. 138, 142.
5. Josiah Royce, *The World and the Individual*, 2d ser., *Nature, Man, and the Moral Order* (New York: The Macmillan Co., 1901), p. 3.
6. John Dewey, *Human Nature and Conduct* (New York: Modern Library, 1930), p. 7.
7. René Descartes, "Discourse on the Method of Rightly Conducting the Reason and Seeking for Truth in the Sciences," in *Descartes: Selections*, ed. Ralph W. Eaton (New York: Charles Scribner's Sons, 1927), pp. 4, 5, 8.
8. Ibid., p. 9.
9. Ibid., p. 13.
10. Ibid., pp. 21, 23.
11. Ibid., p. 24.
12. Immanuel Kant, *Fundamental Principles of the Metaphysics of Morals* (Indianapolis: Bobbs-Merrill Co., 1949), p. 33.
13. The description of essential thinking in "What is Metaphysics?" appears as an aspect of Heidegger's primarily polemical undertaking, which in large part is directed to showing that his thought is not cowardly, but courageous.
14. Martin Heidegger, "What is Metaphysics?," in Heidegger, *Existence and Being*, trans. R. F. C. Hull and Alan Crick (Chicago: Henry Regnery, 1949), p. 353.
15. Ibid., p. 358.
16. Descartes, "Discourse on the Method," p. 28.

17. Jean-Paul Sartre, *The Words* (New York: Fawcett Publications, 1964), p. 159.
18. Ibid., p. 156.
19. Arthur Schopenhauer, *Essay on the Freedom of the Will* (Indianapolis: Bobbs-Merrill Co., 1960), p. 21.

2   JOSIAH ROYCE

1. Josiah Royce, *Lectures on Modern Idealism* (New Haven: Yale University Press, 1919), p. 241.
2. Josiah Royce, *The Religious Aspect of Philosophy: A Critique of the Bases of Conduct and of Faith* (Boston: Houghton Mifflin and Co., 1885), p. 8.
3. Josiah Royce, *The World and the Individual*, 2d ser., *Nature, Man, and the Moral Order* (New York: The Macmillan Co., 1901), p. 2.
4. G. W. F. Hegel, *Reason in History: A General Introduction to the Philosophy of History* (Indianapolis: Bobbs-Merrill Co., 1953), pp. 26, 27.
5. Ibid., p. 27.
6. Royce, *The World*, p. 3.
7. Royce, *The Religious Aspect*, pp. 14, 5.
8. Josiah Royce, "Words of Professor Royce at the Walton Hotel at Philadelphia, December 29, 1915," in *The Basic Writings of Josiah Royce*, ed. John J. McDermott (Chicago: University of Chicago Press, 1969), 1:31, 32, 33.
9. Royce, *The Religious Aspect*, p. 389.
10. Ibid., pp. 389, 424.
11. Royce, *The World*, pp. 25–26.
12. Royce, *The Basic Writings*, pp. 34, 35.
13. Royce, *The Religious Aspect*, pp. 441, 442.
14. Ibid., p. 12.
15. Josiah Royce, *The Problem of Christianity* (1913; reprint ed., Chicago: University of Chicago Press, 1968), pp. 41, 356, 268.
16. Ibid., p. 357.
17. Ibid., p. 362.
18. Royce, *The World*, p. 172.
19. Ibid., p. 429.
20. Dietrich Bonhoeffer, *The Cost of Discipleship* (New York: The Macmillan Co., 1963), pp. 61–86.
21. Josiah Royce, *The Philosophy of Loyalty* (New York: The Macmillan Co., 1908), p. 3.
22. Feodor Dostoevsky, *The Brothers Karamazov* (New York: New American Library, 1957), p. 235.
23. Royce, *The Philosophy of Loyalty*, p. 196.

3   C. S. PEIRCE

1. Josiah Royce, *The Problem of Christianity* (1913; reprint ed., Chicago: University of Chicago Press, 1968), p. 39.
2. Charles S. Peirce, "The Fixation of Belief," in *Collected Papers of Charles Sanders Peirce*, ed. Charles Hartshorne and Paul Weiss, 6 vols. (Cambridge: Harvard University Press, Belknap Press, 1960), vol. 5, *Pragmatism and Pragmaticism*, p. 223 n.

3. Peirce, Preface, in *Collected Papers*, vol. 1, *Principles of Philosophy*, p. x (1.7). References in parentheses are to volume and paragraph of the *Collected Papers*.
4. Peirce, "The Marriage of Religion and Science," in *Collected Papers*, vol. 6, *Scientific Metaphysics*, p. 302 (6.428).
5. Charles S. Peirce, "The Place of Our Age in the History of Civilization," in *Charles S. Peirce: Selected Writings*, ed. Philip P. Wiener (New York: Dover Publications, 1966), pp. 6, 9.
6. Ibid., p. 13.
7. Peirce, "Science and Immortality," in *Collected Papers*, 6:372 (6.553).
8. Peirce, "Evolutionary Love," in *Collected Papers*, 6:190 (6.287), 205 (6.307).
9. Ibid., p. 212 (6.315).
10. Peirce, "The Law of Mind," in *Collected Papers*, 6:103 (6.139).
11. Peirce, "Evolutionary Love," in *Collected Papers*, 6:213, 212–13 (6.315).
12. Peirce, "Notes on Positivism," in *Selected Writings*, p. 139.
13. Peirce, "The Place of Our Age in the History of Civilization," in *Selected Writings*, p. 6.
14. Peirce, "Some Consequences of Four Incapacities," in *Collected Papers*, 5:156 (5.264), 157 (5.265).
15. Peirce, "The Fixation of Belief," in *Collected Papers*, 5:232, 233 n (5.376).
16. Peirce, "The Categories in Detail," in *Collected Papers*, 1:170 (1.336).
17. Peirce, "Some Consequences of Four Incapacities," in *Collected Papers*, 5:156 (5.264), 157 (5.265).
18. Peirce, "The Doctrine of Chances," in *Collected Papers*, vol. 2, *Elements of Logic*, pp. 395–96 (2.652).
19. Ibid., pp. 396 (2.653), 398 (2.654).
20. Ibid., p. 399 (2.654, 655, 656).
21. Peirce, "The Fixation of Belief," in *Collected Papers*, 5:227 (5.366).
22. Peirce, "How to Make our Ideas Clear," in *Collected Papers*, 5:258 n, 259 n (5.402).
23. Feodor Dostoevsky, *The Brothers Karamazov* (New York: New American Library, 1957), pp. 279, 295.
24. Peirce, "How to Make our Ideas Clear," in *Collected Papers*, 5:259 n (5.402).
25. Ibid., pp. 252 (5.393), 253 (5.394).
26. Peirce, "Evolutionary Love," in *Collected Papers*, 6:208 (6.311).
27. Peirce, "What is Christian Faith?" in *Collected Papers*, 6:305 (6.438), 307 (6.445).
28. Peirce, "The Fixation of Belief," in *Collected Papers*, 5:234 (5.377), 227 (5.366).

4 WILLIAM JAMES

1. Charles S. Peirce, "A Survey of Pragmaticism," in *Collected Papers of Charles Sanders Peirce*, ed. Charles Hartshorne and Paul Weiss, 6 vols. (Cambridge: Harvard University Press, Belknap Press, 1960), vol. 5, *Pragmatism and Pragmaticism*, p. 318 (5.467). John Dewey, "What Pragmatism Means by Practical," in Dewey, *The Middle Works, 1899–1924* (Carbondale and Edwardsville: Southern Illinois University Press, 1976–), vol. 4, *1907–1909*, ed. Jo Ann Boydston (1977), pp. 98–115.
2. Peirce, "The Fixation of Belief," in *Collected Papers*, 5:223 n.
3. Josiah Royce, *The Problem of Christianity* (Chicago: University of Chicago Press, 1968), pp. 344, 345.

4. William James, *The Varieties of Religious Experience: A Study in Human Nature* (New York: Longman's Green and Co., 1902), p. 487.
5. Ibid.
6. Ibid., pp. 136 – 37.
7. Ibid., pp. 160, 161.
8. William A. Clebsch, *American Religious Thought: A History* (Chicago: University of Chicago Press, 1973), pp. 138, 142.
9. William James, *The Principles of Psychology* (New York: Henry Holt and Co., 1890), 2:285, 298.
10. Ibid., p. 321.
11. William James, "The Sentiment of Rationality," in James, *The Will to Believe and Other Essays in Popular Philosophy*, ed. Frederick H. Burkhardt, Fredson Bowers, and Ignas K. Skrupskelis (Cambridge: Harvard University Press, 1979), p. 57.
12. Ibid., pp. 58, 63.
13. Ibid., p. 64.
14. Ibid., p. 65.
15. Gay Wilson Allen, *William James: A Biography* (New York: The Viking Press, 1967), pp. 165, 168, 169.
16. James, "The Moral Philosopher and the Moral Life," in *The Will to Believe*, p. 161.
17. William James, "The Will to Believe," in *The Will to Believe*, pp. 13, 20, 29, 30.
18. Ibid., p. 31.
19. Ibid., pp. 27, 29.
20. Ibid., p. 31.
21. Ibid., p. 33.

5   JOHN DEWEY

1. John Dewey, "The Existence of the World as a Logical Problem," in Dewey, *The Middle Works, 1899 – 1924* (Carbondale and Edwardsville: Southern Illinois University Press, 1976 –), vol. 8, *1915*, ed. Jo Ann Boydston (1979), pp. 83, 87, 96.
2. John Dewey, *The Quest for Certainty* (New York: Minton, Balch and Co., 1929), p. 3.
3. Ibid., pp. 6 – 7, 6.
4. For a more complete discussion of false consciousness in idealistic and naturalistic theories, see Deena Weinstein and Michael Weinstein, "The Sociology of Nonknowledge: A Paradigm," in *Research in Sociology of Knowledge, Sciences and Art*, ed. Robert Alun Jones (Greenwich, Conn.: JAI Press, 1978), 1:151 – 66.
5. David F. Swenson, "Objective Uncertainty and Human Faith," *Philosophical Review* 37 (September 1928): 433 – 59. Swenson's argument is particularly interesting because it shows the directions that American thought in its classical period might have gone toward an existentialism.
6. Charles S. Peirce, "Issues of Pragmaticism," in *Collected Papers of Charles Sanders Peirce*, ed. Charles Hartshorne and Paul Weiss, 6 vols. (Cambridge: Harvard University Press, Belknap Press, 1960), vol. 5, *Pragmatism and Pragmaticism*, pp. 293 – 313 (5.438 – 463).
7. Dewey, *The Quest*, pp. 8 – 9.
8. Ibid., pp. 35 – 36, 46.

9. John Dewey, *A Common Faith* (New Haven: Yale University Press, 1934), p. 24.
10. Dewey, *The Quest*, p. 307.
11. Dewey, *A Common Faith*, pp. 25, 26.
12. Ibid., p. 87.
13. John Dewey, "From Absolutism to Experimentalism," in *Contemporary American Philosophy*, ed. George P. Adams and William Pepperell Montague (New York: The Macmillan Co., 1930), 2:27.
14. Dewey, *The Quest*, pp. 307, 308.
15. Ibid., p. 308.
16. Ibid., pp. 311, 37 n.
17. John Dewey, *Liberalism and Social Action* (New York: G. P. Putnam's Sons, 1935).

6   GEORGE SANTAYANA

1. George Santayana, *Character and Opinion in the United States*, in *The Works of George Santayana*, vol. 8, Triton Edition (New York: Charles Scribner's Sons, 1936), p. 3.
2. George Santayana, *Reason in Common Sense*, in Santayana, *The Works of George Santayana*, vol. 3, Triton Edition (New York: Charles Scribner's Sons, 1936), p. 36.
3. Santayana, *Scepticism and Animal Faith*, in Santayana, *The Works of George Santayana*, vol. 13, Triton Edition (New York: Charles Scribner's Sons, 1936), p. 4.
4. Ibid., pp. 99, 7.
5. Santayana, *Character*, in *Works*, 8:42, 43.
6. Ibid., p. 48.
7. William James, *Pragmatism*, ed. Fredson Bowers and Ignas Skrupskelis (Cambridge: Harvard University Press, 1975), p. 125.
8. Santayana, *Character*, in *Works*, 8:75, 76.
9. Ibid., p. 76.
10. Santayana, *Reason*, in *Works*, 3:20.
11. George Santayana, "George Santayana on Existentialism: An Unpublished Letter," *Partisan Review* 25 (Fall 1958): 635, 637.
12. Ibid., p. 635.
13. Santayana, *Scepticism*, in *Works*, 13:8, 101, 99.
14. Ibid., p. 100.
15. Ibid., pp. 191–92, 76, 192.
16. Santayana, *Reason*, in *Works*, 3:4.
17. George Santayana, *Three Philosophical Poets*, in Santayana, *The Works of George Santayana*, vol. 6, Triton Edition (New York: Charles Scribner's Sons, 1936), p. 13.
18. Santayana, *Character*, in *Works*, 8:25, 118.
19. George Santayana, *Dominations and Powers* (New York: Charles Scribner's Sons, 1951), p. 435.
20. Santayana, *Character*, in *Works*, 8:117, 128, 129, 130.
21. Ibid., pp. 119–20.

7   AMERICAN PHILOSOPHY AND MODERN INDIVIDUALISM

1. Friedrich Nietzsche, *Twilight of the Idols and the Anti-Christ* (Hammondsworth: Penguin Books, 1968), p. 124.
2. Friedrich Nietzsche, *The Birth of Tragedy* (Garden City: Doubleday and Co., 1956), pp. 138, 139, 140.
3. Jean-Paul Sartre, *Nausea* (New York: New Directions, 1964), pp. 172, 170.
4. Karl Jaspers, *Man in the Modern Age* (Garden City: Doubleday and Co., 1957), p. 176.
5. George Santayana, "Character and Opinion in the United States," in *The Works of George Santayana*, vol. 8, Triton Edition (New York: Charles Scribner's Sons, 1936), pp. 71, 26.
6. William James, "The Moral Philosopher and the Moral Life," in James, *The Will to Believe and Other Essays in Popular Philosophy*, ed. Frederick H. Burkhardt, Fredson Bowers, and Ignas K. Skrupskelis (Cambridge: Harvard University Press, 1979), p. 161.
7. Walter Jackson Bate, *Prefaces to Criticism* (Garden City: Doubleday and Co., 1959), p. 209.
8. Harry Levin, "Irving Babbitt and the Teaching of Literature," Irving Babbitt Inaugural Lecture, Harvard University (November 7, 1960), pp. 7, 19.
9. J. David Hoeveler, Jr., *The New Humanism: A Critique of Modern America 1900 – 1940* (Charlottesville: University Press of Virginia, 1977), pp. viii, 41.
10. Ibid., p. 42.
11. Ibid., p. 13.
12. Irving Babbitt, *Rousseau and Romanticism* (Boston and New York: Houghton Mifflin Co., 1919), p. x.
13. Ibid., pp. x, xii.
14. Ibid., p. xiii.
15. Ibid., pp. 259, 300 – 301, 286.
16. Ibid., pp. 161, 178 – 79, 201, 34.
17. Ibid., pp. 369, 370.
18. Ibid., pp. 346, 366.

Name Index

Subject Index